Collins

Your
BOOK TWO

Choice

JOHN FOSTER & SIMON FOSTER

Collins

William Collins' dream of knowledge for all began with the publication of his first book in 1819.

A self-educated mill worker, he not only enriched millions of lives, but also founded a flourishing publishing house. Today, staying true to this spirit, Collins books are packed with inspiration, innovation and practical expertise. They place you at the centre of a world of possibility and give you exactly what you need to explore it.

Collins. Freedom to teach.

Published by Collins

An imprint of HarperCollins*Publishers*

The News Building
1 London Bridge Street
London
SE1 9GF

HarperCollins *Publishers*
Macken House, 39/40 Mayor Street Upper,
Dublin 1, D01 C9W8, Ireland

> **Browse the complete Collins catalogue at**
> **www.collins.co.uk**

British Library Cataloguing in Publication Data

A catalogue record for this publication is available from the British Library.

The publishers would like to thank the following for their help in reviewing the series:
- Jo Fliski, formerly Head of PSHE and English teacher at Lliswerry High School, Newport
- Jo Haycock, Psychology teacher at Sir John Talbot's School, Whitchurch, Shropshire and formerly PSHE Coordinator at Newport Girls' High School
- Tara Mellor, teacher of PSHE, Citizenship and Law, The Mirfield Free Grammar and Sixth Form
- Cat Crossley, diversity consultant and publisher.

Series editor: John Foster
Development editor: Jo Kemp
Commissioning editor: Catherine Martin
Copyeditor: Jo Kemp
Proofreader: Emily Hooton
Cover designer: The Big Mountain
Concept designer: The Big Mountain
Internal designer / Typesetter: 2Hoots Publishing Services Ltd
Permissions researcher: Rachel Thorne
Production controller: Katharine Willard

Printed and bound in the UK by Ashford Colour Press Ltd.

Contents

Introduction

Your Choice Book 2 is the second of three books which together form a comprehensive course in Personal, Social and Health Education (PSHE), including Relationships and Sex Education (RSE) and Health Education, at Key Stage 3. The table shows how the topics covered fit within four strands – Personal wellbeing and mental health, Relationships and sex, Social education and Physical health and wellbeing – to provide a coherent course in RSE and PSHE for students in Year 8.

The units provide you with key information on relevant topics and the various activities provide opportunities for you to share your views and to develop your own opinions.

Throughout the book there are discussion activities that involve you in learning how to work as a team and how to develop the skills of co-operation and negotiation. You are presented with situations in which you must work with others, to analyse information, to consider what actions you could take and to make choices and decisions.

Personal wellbeing and mental health

These units focus on on increasing your self-awareness, learning to manage your emotions, banking and saving money, and dealing with stress.

1. You and adolescence
11. Managing your emotions
12. Managing stress
13. You and your money
17. You and your future

Relationships and sex education

These units concentrate on consent, making you aware of your rights and responsibilities in relationships, safer sex and STIs, and how to protect yourself on social media, online and in the offline world.

2. You and your relationships
3. Sexual relationships – your responsibilities
4. You and safer sex
5. Staying safe from abuse

Each lesson has a clear focus.

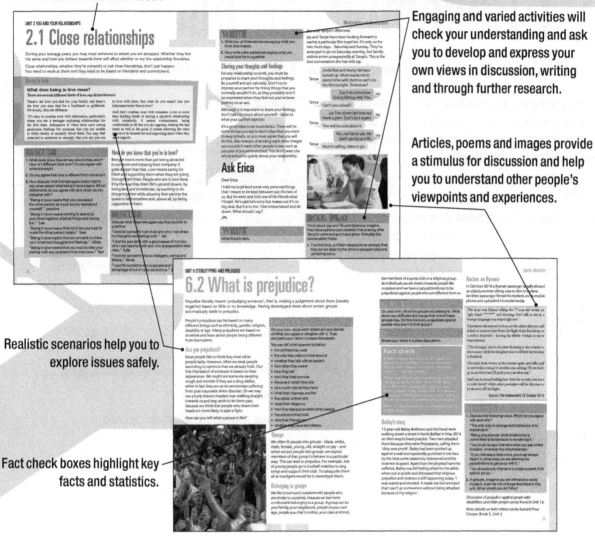

Engaging and varied activities will check your understanding and ask you to develop and express your own views in discussion, writing and through further research.

Articles, poems and images provide a stimulus for discussion and help you to understand other people's viewpoints and experiences.

Realistic scenarios help you to explore issues safely.

Fact check boxes highlight key facts and statistics.

Physical health and wellbeing

These units focus on taking care of your body and on drug awareness, including information about the risks involved in drinking alcohol and using cannabis and MDMA.

7. Drugs and addictions
8. You and alcohol
9. You and your health
10. Caring for your body

Social education

These units explore attitudes to teenagers, older people and people with disabilities, and introduce Citizenship topics such as children's rights, relations with the police, and your opinions on social issues.

6. Stereotyping and prejudice
14. The police and the law
15. You as a citizen
16. You and other people

1.1 Becoming an adult

Adolescence is the period during which a person develops from a child into an adult.

Many changes occur between the ages of 10 and 19 – intellectual and social, physical and psychological – as adolescents mature and establish their adult identity.

Teenagers' rights

Your rights are the things that you are morally or legally entitled to do or have. A group of teenagers were asked what rights they thought they should have. Here is a list of some of their answers.

About privacy and their room:

I have the right to …

- *privacy – to stay in my room alone and to say whether anyone can come in.*
- *choose whether to tidy my room.*
- *play on the computer for as long as I want.*

About their health and sexuality:

I have the right to …

- *take responsibility for my own health care.*
- *decide for myself whether or not to see my doctor.*
- *visit a family planning or sexual health clinic without telling my parents or carers.*
- *have my sexuality accepted and respected.*

About their day-to-day life:

I have the right to …

- *have essentials paid for by my parents/carer.*
- *have my clothes washed and ironed for me.*
- *have my meals cooked for me.*
- *be given pocket money.*
- *be paid for any chores I do.*
- *be given my own mobile phone.*

About their opinions:

I have the right to …

- *have my own opinions.*
- *be listened to.*

About making their own choices:

I have the right to …

- *choose which school I go to.*
- *choose for myself which subjects I study.*
- *choose my own clothes.*
- *choose whether or not I drink alcohol.*
- *decide whether to become a vegetarian or vegan.*
- *choose my own friends.*
- *decide whether or not to have sex with my boyfriend/girlfriend.*

About making their own decisions:

I have the right to …

- *decide for myself what time I have to come in.*
- *go where I want when I want.*
- *stay out all night if I want to.*

YOUR CHOICE

Study the list. Work in pairs to decide which things you think are rights and which are not rights. Suggest any rights you think should be added to the list.

WRITE

Put the list of what you have decided are your rights as a teenager in order of importance. Write a paragraph saying why you have put them in that order and how you feel when one of your rights is denied you.

Parents' and carers' rights

A group of parents and carers of teenagers drew up the following list of rights they thought they should have.

Your parents or carers have the right to …

- *expect you to express your views in a civil manner.*
- *ask you where you are going, when you are going out and who you are going with.*
- *go into your room at any time.*
- *impose a curfew for when you must be in by.*
- *ground you as a punishment.*
- *limit the time you spend on the computer or on your phone each night.*
- *expect you to tidy your room.*
- *choose which school you go to.*
- *choose which subjects you study.*
- *know if you go to a family planning or sexual health clinic.*
- *expect you to participate in family gatherings.*
- *expect you to do your share of chores.*
- *choose not to give you any pocket money.*
- *be present when you see a doctor.*

DISCUSS

In pairs, list which of the rights you think parents or carers have and which they do not. Then compare your lists of parents' rights and teenagers' rights in a class discussion.

Fact check

Teenagers have the right to visit a doctor, family planning or sexual health clinic without their parents being informed.

Pria's problem

Pria says, 'My problem is that my parents want to know where I am all the time. And I mean ALL the time. My mum was so paranoid about me going down the town with my friends on my own when I was younger that she made me wear this tracking device, so she could see where I was and know what I was doing. She said it gave her peace of mind.

The Gator, a GPS tracking device that can be worn on your wrist.

'My friends thought it was an invasion of my privacy. One of them even suggested that I take it off and throw it away. Another one suggested that I should let her wear it for a while and see what happened. I said, "No way!" My mum would have been so upset with me.

'I'm 13 now and my mum wants me to go on wearing it. I've tried to explain that I didn't mind wearing it when I was younger, but that now I'm a teenager I want to be independent and not to have her checking up on me all the time. It's as though she doesn't trust me.'

Pria's mother says that she is only doing it to protect her daughter. She says, 'There are so many dangers out there. Knowing where she is means that I can keep an eye on her. It's not easy being a parent these days. I know what I was like when I was her age. So many parents let their kids do whatever they want. It's no wonder so many of them get into trouble.'

DISCUSS

1. In groups, discuss what Pria and her mother say.

   a) Is asking Pria to wear a GPS tracking device an 'invasion of her privacy'?

   b) Why does her mother want her to wear one?

   c) At what age should parents allow you to go out where and when you like?

2. Read the two viewpoints below. Discuss why you agree or disagree with them.

   'Teenagers aren't aware of the dangers that are out there. They don't realise that parents are only concerned about their safety.'

   'The problem is that parents worry too much. They interfere in teenagers' lives and try to control them.'

1.2 Problems with parents

One way of resolving the differences that can cause conflict between you and your parents or carers is to draw up a contract stating how they expect you to behave and how you expect them to behave.

Here is part of the contract that Marcia (14) drew up with her parents:

> We agree that Marcia can go and stay overnight at a friend's house provided that it is arranged beforehand and that we are given the friend's name, address and telephone number.
>
> Marcia also agrees that, if she is going round to a friend's straight from school, she will check that it's all right and will be back no later than 6 p.m.
>
> Marcia agrees to help clean the house, including the bathroom and toilet, once a week in return for £2.50 extra pocket money.

WRITE

Draft details of other things that Marcia and her parents might include in the contract, for example about respecting her privacy and taking responsibility for seeing that she has clean clothes.

DISCUSS

Discuss the advice Louisa Fairbanks gives below. Which do you think are the three most useful pieces of advice?

Top tips on talking with parents

As you seek to be more independent, you may find yourself arguing with your parents. **Louisa Fairbanks** offers some tips on how to have meaningful conversations.

1   There are two sides to every argument. Try to see it from your parents' or carers' point of view. For example, you want to go on a sleepover. Do they know the person? Have they met the friend's parents? Your parents and carers are concerned for your safety. What can you do or say to reassure them that you will be all right?

2   Be prepared to negotiate and meet them half way. For example, it's Sunday and you want to go out but you haven't done your homework. You say you'll do it when you get back at 7 p.m. Your parents want you home by 5 p.m. Would it be better to settle for 6 p.m. and meet them in the middle?

3   Don't be defensive about your views. State them clearly and firmly.

4   Don't ridicule your parents' or carers' standpoint. Listen to what they have to say. Treat them with the respect you expect them to show you.

5   If you are discussing something you feel strongly about, such as women's rights, homophobia or immigration, don't back down.

6   Make requests politely. Ask for the things you want. Don't demand them.

7   Pick the right moment. However much you want something, when your parent or carer comes in after a long day at work may not be the best time to ask if they will lend you the money to buy a new game. Waiting till they've had something to eat might be a better idea.

8   Make statements beginning with 'I' rather than 'you'. For example, say, 'I feel I am not being listened to' rather than 'You aren't listening' or 'You don't understand.'

9   Keep calm. Storming out of the room won't solve anything. If you feel the argument is becoming too heated and going nowhere, suggest that you take a break. Agree that you'll discuss the matter later.

10   Keep the statements in the positive. It's better to agree, 'I **will** be back on time' rather than 'I **won't** stay out too late.'

Who's responsible?

How much do you really do for yourself? Teenagers often complain that their parents won't let them lead their own lives. Then they complain when things aren't done for them. Here is a list of the sort of things that need to be done in most households.

- Tidying your room.
- Washing your clothes.
- Arranging to have your hair cut.
- Buying your toothpaste and toiletries.
- Paying for your mobile phone.
- Preparing your packed lunch.
- Looking after the family's pet.
- Cleaning your shoes or sports kit.
- Checking that your bike is safe to ride.
- Cooking some meals.
- Vacuuming your room.
- Changing your sheets and duvet cover.

Whose responsibility is it to keep your room tidy?

YOUR CHOICE

Study the list above and write down who you think should be responsible for each action and who in your home actually does it. What does this tell you about how responsible you are at home?

Accepting responsibility

Being an adult means accepting responsibility, says Eileen Pickersgill.

Part of becoming an adult means learning to take responsibility for your actions. For example, if you forget to go to an appointment at the hairdressers, don't expect someone else to ring up and apologise. It's up to you to phone and make another appointment. Similarly, if you lose or break something, it's up to you to sort it out and to offer to pay for a replacement. In the past, you may have relied on a parent or carer to help you out. But if you want to be independent then it's up to you take responsibility for what you do. The more you act responsibly, the more freedom you will be given.

Zara's problem

Zara is ready to go home from a birthday party. She has agreed to be in by 9 p.m. and to walk home with Sam, who only lives a few doors away. The walk home will only take 15 minutes. It's now 8.45 p.m. Zara tells Sam that it's time to leave, but Sam wants to stay on for another half-hour. Sam says her parents won't mind.

DISCUSS

1. Do you agree with what Eileen Pickersgill says about taking responsibility for your actions?

2. Zara has the following options:
   - stay on and wait for Sam
   - try to persuade Sam to come with her
   - walk home alone
   - phone her dad to come and fetch her.
   a) What would be the most responsible thing for Zara to do?
   b) What would be the consequences of each action?

1.3 Being responsible

As a teenager you are faced with many choices. It is important to make informed, safe and healthy decisions. By showing responsibility, you will demonstrate that you are ready to have greater freedom and independence.

Take control of your life

If you are to become an independent adult and eventually move out and live your own life, you'll have to do things for yourself, such as cooking meals and washing and ironing your clothes.

- You need to take responsibility for your appearance and your personal hygiene. For example, making sure you wash or shower regularly and clean your teeth.
- It's worth learning how to cook and how to wash and iron your clothes.
- If you want your room to be your private place, you need to keep it clean and change the sheets and duvet cover.
- Don't leave all the household tasks to other people. Show that you're responsible by doing your fair share of household chores.
- As a young adult you will want to start to take responsibility for your own health. It is important to know certain things about your health in order to take responsibility for it (see Unit 9).

Take control of your money

Handle your money responsibly (see Unit 13).

- Work out your income and your expenses.
- Don't borrow money you can't afford to pay back.
- Don't expect your parents to help you out if you overspend.

RESEARCH

On your own, study the health checklist opposite.

1. Do you have all the information that you need to know? How could you fill in any gaps?
2. Create a factsheet containing the information.

My health checklist

- My GP's name, address and telephone number and how to make an appointment by phone or online.
- Name and address of the nearest pharmacy where I can get prescriptions.
- Details of the nearest hospital with an Accident and Emergency department.
- My national health number and where my national health card is kept.
- Immunisations I have had and any I am due to have in the future.
- Any allergies I have, for example nut allergy.
- Any medical conditions I have and medicines I take for them, for example asthma.
- Any childhood illnesses I have had, for example chicken pox.

What I regret most

A group of 20-year-olds say what they regret most about what they did in their teenage years.

- Not listening to my parents: 'I argued and got angry with them. But they were there when I got into trouble.' **Nadia**
- Trying to be popular: 'I went out of my way to fit in and did some things I'm ashamed of. I once lied and allowed someone else to be punished for what I'd done.' **Finn**
- Neglecting my schoolwork: 'It was only when I started applying for jobs that I realised I had wasted the opportunity that school offered. If I had paid more attention I wouldn't have had to retake my GCSE Maths.' **Hassan**
- Not asking for help: 'I got very depressed but refused to let anyone help me even though I was struggling to cope.' **Charlie**

- Being selfish: 'I was so busy worrying about myself that I didn't notice how much hurt I was causing others by my actions. There was this girl who was lonely and tried to make friends with me, but I shut her out and ignored her.' **Gemma**
- Starting to smoke: 'I started smoking because everyone in our group did. Now I'm hooked on nicotine.' **Petra**

DISCUSS

Discuss the regrets these people have and the reasons for them. What can you learn from their experiences?

Think about the future

Now is the time to start thinking about your future. You may already have a clear idea of what you want to do as a career, the exams you'll need to pass and the qualifications you'll need to get. That's great. But many of you won't have a clear goal and even those of you who think you know may change your minds. So it's worth thinking about the skills you have and your particular strengths, to explore which careers might suit you.

'I'm outgoing and get on with people. I'm fairly well organised and don't mind people telling me what to do. I think I'd fit in well in a shop or office as one of a team. I'm going to do Business Studies at GCSE, which may give me more of an idea of what's out there.' **Max**

'I've got a good memory and my science teacher says I've got good research skills. I'm good at making observations and organising information. I'm investigating what qualifications I'd need to do laboratory work of some kind.' **Adeena**

DISCUSS

In pairs, each choose one or two jobs from this list:
- lawyer
- lifeguard
- nursery nurse
- travel rep
- doctor
- hotel receptionist
- architect
- journalist
- photographer
- shop assistant
- engineer
- pharmacist
- social worker
- gym instructor.

Study the table below and discuss the type of skills you think would be required in those jobs.

WRITE

1. Think of a situation where you have used or developed skills in any areas listed in the table. Write them down.

2. Write about the skills you have and how they might fit a career, similar to the statements made by Max and Adeena above.

3. Write a letter to your future self, aged 21. Think about what you will have done by then. How will your life have changed? What will you have achieved?

Types of skill				
People skills	**Thinking skills**	**Using information**	**Helping people to get things done**	**Seeing things from a different angle**
Communication	Evaluating	Memorising	Coordinating and liaising	Thinking laterally
Inspiration	Problem solving	Researching		Flair and imagination
Negotiation	Prioritising	Record keeping	Overseeing	Seeing potential
Appreciation	Weighing up evidence and alternatives	Calculating	Planning	Finding links
Delegation		Classifying/organising information	Recognising other people's talents/skills	Seeing relationships/ connections
Determination		Observing		
Advising				

2.1 Close relationships

During your teenage years, you may meet someone to whom you are attracted. Whether they feel the same and how you behave towards them will affect whether or not the relationship flourishes.

Close relationships, whether they're romantic or just close friendships, don't just happen. You need to work at them and they need to be based on friendship and commitment.

Being in love

What does being in love mean?

There are several different kinds of love, says Erica Stewart.

There's the love you feel for your family and there's the love you may feel for someone you are seeing or dating. Obviously, they are different.

It's easy to confuse love with infatuation, particularly when you are a teenager exploring relationships for the first time. Infatuation is when have such strong passionate feelings for someone that you are unable to think clearly or sensibly about them. You may feel attracted to someone so strongly that you say you are in love with them. But what do you mean? Are you infatuated rather than in love?

And don't confuse love with romance. Love is more than holding hands or having a physical relationship with somebody. It means commitment, being comfortable in all that you do together, sharing the bad times as well as the good. It means allowing the other person to be themselves and supporting them when they need support.

DISCUSS

1. What does Erica Stewart say about infatuation? How is it different from love? Do you agree with what she says?

2. Do you agree that love is different from romance?

3. Now discuss what the teenagers below had to say when asked what being in love means. Which statements do you agree with and which do you disagree with?

‘Being in love means that you care about the other person as much as you care about yourself.’ **Jasmine**

‘Being in love means wanting to spend all your time together, sharing things and having fun.’ **Leo**

‘Being in love means that you'll do your best to make the other person happy.’ **Sam**

‘Being in love means that you are able to share your innermost thoughts and feelings.’ **Olivia**

‘Being in love means that you want to help your partner with any problems they may have.’ **Ted**

How do you know that you're in love?

Being in love is more than just being attracted to someone and enjoying their company. It goes deeper than that. Love means caring for them and supporting them when they are going through bad times. People who are in love show it by the way they share life's ups and downs, by being kind and considerate, by wanting to do things together while allowing their partner the space to be themselves and, above all, by being supportive of them.

DISCUSS

Discuss what these teenagers say they look for in a partner.

‘I look for someone I can trust and who I can share my thoughts and feelings with.’ **Abi**

‘I look for someone with a good sense of humour, who I can have fun with and who is prepared to take risks.’ **Kyle**

‘I look for someone who is intelligent, caring and listens.’ **Noah**

‘I look for someone who is sincere and won't take advantage of me or try to control me.’ **Zoe**

WRITE

1. Write two or three sentences saying what you think love means.

2. Now write a few sentences saying what you would look for in a partner.

Sharing your thoughts and feelings

For any relationship to work, you must be prepared to share your thoughts and feelings. Be yourself and act naturally. Don't try to impress your partner by doing things that you normally wouldn't do, as they probably won't be impressed when they find out you've been putting on an act.

Although it is important to share your feelings, don't talk too much about yourself – listen to what your partner says too.

It's a good idea to set boundaries. There will be some things you say to each other that you want to keep private, so you must agree that you will do this. Also beware of sending each other images you wouldn't want other people to see, such as pictures of you semi-clothed. You don't want the whole school to gossip about your relationship.

Ask Erica

Dear Erica

I told my boyfriend some very personal things that I meant to be kept between just the two of us. But he went and told one of his friends what I'd said. He's said he's sorry but makes out it's no big deal. But it is to me. I feel embarrassed and let down. What should I say?

Jon

WRITE

Write Erica's reply.

Jay and Tanya's dilemma

Jay and Tanya have been looking forward to seeing a particular film together. It's only on for two more days – Saturday and Sunday. They've arranged to go on Saturday evening, but family visitors arrive unexpectedly at Tanya's. This is the text conversation she has with Jay.

Tanya: Uncle Rob and Aunty Val have turned up. Mum wants me to spend time with them so can't do the film tonight. Tomorrow?

Jay: Can't do tomorrow. Going fishing with Trev.

Tanya: Can't you cancel?

Jay: Let Trev down last time we made a plan. Can't do it again.

Tanya: Trev will be cool about it.

Jay: No, not fair to ask. His dad's giving us a lift.

Tanya: Mum's calling. Have to go.

ROLE PLAY

Think about Jay and Tanya's dilemma. Imagine they have a phone conversation that evening after Tanya's uncle and aunt have gone. Role play the conversation twice.

1. The first time, put their viewpoints so strongly that they do not listen to the other's viewpoint and end up having a row.

2. Then repeat it with them listening to each other's viewpoint and trying to reach a compromise.

2.2 What makes a healthy relationship?

How you behave towards your partner or towards your best friends can help to determine the kind of relationship you have and whether or not it is healthy.

Keys to a healthy relationship

There are a few key things that will help you to have healthy relationships.

Trust

The most important thing in a healthy relationship is trust. You feel completely confident that your partner or best friend will not let you down. You feel you can tell them anything about how you feel and they will not repeat it to anyone else. You can rely on them to support you. And they feel the same way about you.

Space

Your partner or best friend allows you to be yourself. They don't expect you to be with them all the time. They accept the fact that there are times when you will want to be with other friends and your family. They recognise that you have other interests that you want to keep up and they encourage you to do so. And you do the same for them.

Communication

You say what you think and feel. You don't hold back from saying things because you are afraid of how your partner or best friend will react. But you make sure you say things sensitively so as not to hurt their feelings. You listen to what your partner or friend has to say and your partner or friend listens to you.

Compromise

If you think differently about an issue, you are both willing to meet halfway and reach a compromise even though you both feel strongly about it.

Respect

You respect each other's feelings and views, even when you disagree. You accept that you are both entitled to set boundaries, for example in a sexual relationship.

Adam's story

Adam is a passionate supporter of animal rights. A protest is to take place at a research laboratory. He asks his friend Callum to go with him. Callum doesn't really want to go as he is afraid there will be trouble. He doesn't like Harry who is organising the protest and doesn't trust him. But Callum doesn't want it to affect his friendship with Adam.

ROLE PLAY

Discuss what Callum might say to Adam. Role play the conversation.

Top tips for good relationships

1. Show your friend that you care. Take an interest in what they say and do. Listen to them when they tell you about what's going on in their life. Be kind and considerate. When you are discussing what to do together, don't expect to have your own way all the time.

2. Encourage them to pursue their interests. Don't expect them to give up an activity they enjoy. Go and support them, for example if they play a sport, sing in a choir or act in a play.

3. Don't be jealous of them having other friends – accept that they'll want to have other friends, and so should you. Don't expect them to spend all their time with you.

4. Show appreciation. Let your friend know that you value their friendship by thanking them when they do something for you.

5. Keep your promises. If your friend tells you something in confidence, keep it to yourself. Relationships are built on trust. Don't betray your friend's trust by talking about them behind their back.

6. Handle quarrels calmly and maturely – all friends have times when they quarrel. Don't get angry. Keep calm. Explain why you feel as you do and listen to their explanation of why they feel as they do. Reach a compromise if you can. If you can't, then agree to differ.

7. If you have behaved badly towards them, apologise for your bad behaviour. But just saying you are sorry isn't enough – make sure it's a sincere apology and show the change in your behaviour.

8. Stand by your friend. When the going gets tough, and your friend is upset or worried, help them by letting them know that you are there for them.

9. Be honest. Say what you think and feel, but in a considerate way. Don't pretend. Respect the other person's opinions.

10. Have fun. Make sure you do things together that you both enjoy, such as going to the cinema, for a bike ride or to a fun fair.

YOUR CHOICE

1. In pairs, identify and rank your top three suggestions from the list above.

2. Then compare your answers in groups. Give reasons for your views.

2.3 Unhealthy relationships and feelings of rejection

Some relationships formed when we are teenagers last into adulthood, but many do not. When a relationship breaks down, either with a romantic partner or a best friend, you may experience feelings of rejection.

What are the signs of an unhealthy relationship?

Control

Your partner or best friend insists on making all the decisions. They insist that you spend all your spare time together. The relationship is suffocating and you are not able pursue your own interests.

Blame

Your partner or best friend makes you feel that you are spoiling their life and that you are responsible for everything that is going wrong in it.

Threats

Your partner or best friend threatens to harm themselves if you don't do what they want. They use emotional blackmail to get what they want from you.

Betrayal

Your partner or best friend lies to you about where they have been and what they have been doing. They tell other people things about you that you expected them to keep between the two of you. They are two-faced, talking about you behind your back.

Jealousy

Your partner or best friend is jealous of you spending time with your friends and family. They don't like it when you text your other friends or hang out with them. They are possessive and want you all to themselves.

Put-downs

Instead of celebrating your achievements, your partner or best friend belittles them. They may make remarks about you and your family behind your back. They may deliberately humiliate you in front of your friends and even spread unkind rumours.

Unpredictability

You cannot tell how your partner or best friend will behave towards you. Their mood swings one way and then another. One minute they might be kind and considerate, the next completely lose their temper.

Physical violence

Your partner or best friend lashes out at you, then begs for your forgiveness.

Refusal to discuss problems

Every time you try to have a serious conversation with them, your partner or best friend refuses to listen and dismisses your concerns. It is impossible to pin them down and talk about problems.

YOUR CHOICE

Talk about each of the behaviours above.

1. Which do you think are the most damaging to a relationship?

2. Pick out the three you think are the most damaging and say why.

WRITE

Write a 200-word article for a teenage magazine entitled, 'How to spot the signs of an unhealthy relationship'.

Ask Erica

Dear Erica

I told my boyfriend that I couldn't go out with him on Saturday afternoon because it was my friend's birthday. But the real reason was that I'd arranged to go out with another boy. I'm worried that someone from school may have seen us and that he'll find out. What should I do?

Aisha

Dear Aisha

Trust is an essential ingredient in a successful relationship. You need to ask yourself why you wanted to go out with someone else. Is it because your relationship with your boyfriend is coming to an end? Were you flattered that someone else had asked you out? Why are you worried that your boyfriend might find out? Why are you keeping it secret from him? Answering these questions will help you decide what to do.

Erica

DISCUSS

Discuss Aisha's dilemma and Erica's reply.

- What could be the consequences of Aisha telling her boyfriend?
- What could be the consequences of her remaining silent?
- Should she have told her boyfriend the truth before she went out with someone else?

Ask Erica

Dear Erica

The boy I'm going out with wants to spend every minute of every day with me. He's so controlling. He always wants me to do things with him. He doesn't give me any space. I'm afraid my friends are going to give up on me because I never go out with them. What should I do?

Iris

WRITE

Write Erica's reply to Iris.

Feeling rejected

There are many reasons why relationships, with a partner, a best friend or a group of friends, come to an end. While this can feel like the end of the world at the time, it is important to realise that the feelings are temporary and will change. You may feel rejected in the short term, but you will eventually feel better in the long term.

Advice on feeling rejected

'Losing a friend can be like the grief you feel when someone has died – you go through a similar grief cycle. The best thing to do is to recognise this and work through your feelings – time is a great healer.' **Megan**

'The important thing is not to feel alone, but to talk things through with a friend, teacher, sibling or parent.' **Abdul**

'You may not be right for a particular person at a particular time, but you will be right for somebody else. Most people have a number of relationships, have different close friends and change friendship groups as they go through life.' **Jane**

'Being alone is OK. Take some time out for yourself to get over a relationship before starting a new one.' **Jacob**

'What's important is how you feel inside. Remember that you are unique. Go and have an ice cream, watch a good film or go out with other friends who are there to support you.' **Hannah**

YOUR CHOICE

1. In pairs, rank the advice above in order from best to worst.
2. Then compare your answers in groups.
3. What other advice would you give to someone who is feeling rejected? Give reasons for your views.

3.1 Giving your consent

Consent is when you agree to take part in an activity and your partner agrees too.

Consent is necessary for hugging, kissing and touching, as well as for sexual activity including oral, anal and vaginal sex.

Fact check

According to the law, consent is agreement which is given willingly and freely without threat or fear, and by a person who has the capacity to give their agreement.

Having the capacity to give your agreement means you are old enough to consent (16 or over in the UK) and in a fit state to give your consent – not drunk, asleep or unconscious, or under the influence of drugs.

Any sexual activity without consent is illegal, whatever your age.

If someone forces you to have penetrative sex, they would be guilty of rape. If they touch you without your consent, they would be guilty of sexual assault.

Five things you should know about consent

1. **Consent must be clear and explicit –** You can't just assume that your partner is comfortable about kissing you and letting you touch them or having sex with you. The only way you can be certain that they give their consent is to ask them.

2. **Consent can be withdrawn** – At any point during sexual activity, your partner can change their mind if they are not comfortable with what you are doing or suggesting. They can withdraw their consent and tell you to stop. If you continue, you are committing an offence. When a person asks you to stop during a sexual activity, you must stop at once.

3. **Consent must be given freely** – You must not put any pressure on your partner. If someone gives in and agrees to have sex because they are under pressure, it is not consent.

4. **Consent doesn't last forever** – Just because someone agrees to a sexual activity on one occasion, it doesn't mean they give their permission to doing it again. They may not have enjoyed it or they may not feel like doing it again. You need to check that they are willing to give their consent again.

5. **Drink and drugs affect consent** – If a person has been drinking or taking drugs, it can affect their thinking. A person who is drunk is unable to give their permission for any sexual activity. The same applies to someone who is high on drugs. Legal consent is sober consent.

Asking for consent

You need to check that your partner is giving their consent by asking them.

You need to know what your partner is thinking and feeling, so it's vital to talk before and during any sexual activity.

You can ask for consent before you start by saying things like, 'Do you want to …?', 'How do you feel about …?' and 'Would you like to …?'

You can check that your partner gives consent to what you are doing by asking, 'Do you like this?', 'Shall we …?', 'Can I …?' and 'Do you want me to stop?'

You should also look for signs the other person might be feeling uncomfortable. The following may show someone is not happy about what is happening:

*   they stop kissing you

*   they pull or turn away from you

*   they don't seem to want to be touched

*   they stop speaking or responding

*   they avoid eye contact

*   they look tense or nervous.

If you are in any doubt, ask the other person whether they are happy to continue.

Saying 'No'

Whether the person in question is a complete stranger, someone you met at a party, your best friend or your partner, it is always okay to say no.

Firmly and politely tell the other person that you don't want to have sex or do whatever they are suggesting. How you say this may depend on the situation and the person, but you should not feel you have to explain yourself.

If someone says no to you, respect their feelings and don't put pressure on them to say yes – accept that no means no.

Scenario 1

Jo went out with her friends to a party. A boy she knew came up behind her and slapped her bottom. She is annoyed and embarrassed.

Scenario 2

Finn is at a party. He is sitting next to a boy who puts his hand on Finn's knee and starts to stroke his thigh. Finn isn't sure how he feels about what is happening.

Scenario 3

Evan is at a club. A girl comes and sits down beside him and puts her arm round him and says she's seen him about and she'd like to get to know him.

Scenario 4

Cillian is at a party. He's talking to a girl he likes and wants to kiss her.

DISCUSS

1. Discuss what you think the person should do or say in each situation.

2. Would it make a difference if any of the people were drunk, or if they already knew each other?

Give reasons for your views.

WRITE

Create a podcast for teenagers about what consent means and how to ask for it.

3.2 Am I ready to have sex?

It's your choice whether you feel ready to explore sex with someone else.

You may have talked to friends about it and some of them may have boasted about what they have done. But everyone should make their own decision about when they are ready to have sex and not worry what other people think.

Fact check

Remember that the age of consent is 16.

Deciding whether you are ready to take things further

People may decide to begin having sex for a variety of reasons. If you're considering this yourself, it is important that you think things through to make the right choice for you.

Here are some things young people have said about why they want to take this step.

- I'm doing this to please myself.
- I'm doing this because I want my partner to like me.
- I'm afraid we'll split up if we don't.
- I'm curious to find out what sex feels like.
- I hope it will make us feel closer as a couple.
- All my friends say they have done it.
- My partner keeps asking me to.
- I feel comfortable with this person and can talk to them about contraception and protecting ourselves against STIs.
- I like being with this person and we both feel ready to take things further.

YOUR CHOICE

Read the statements on the left and discuss these questions in a small group.

1. Which do you think are positive reasons for deciding to have sex with someone?

2. Which do you think are not good reasons for deciding to take things further?

Now report back to the class. Were there any statements that you disagreed about? Why?

Sex and peer pressure

Derek Stuart has spoken to a group of older teenagers about the pressures they felt under to have sex.

He found that when asked why they first chose to have sex, girls were more likely than boys to say that they consented because they were in love. Boys, on the other hand, gave answers like, 'I wanted to see what it was like' and, 'So that we could have fun'.

Both boys and girls said that they were under pressure from their peers. Girls said that most of their friends claimed to have lost their virginity and they didn't want to be the odd one out. They also felt under pressure from their partners, making comments such as, 'I was afraid if I didn't have sex with them that we would break up and they'd find another girl who would.' Boys were influenced by the way people in the group boasted about what they had done. 'I wanted them to accept me' was a common reason given.

'I desperately wanted to belong in the group,' said Dave, 'so I made out to my girlfriend that we should try it because I was so into her. She was furious when I told my mates that we'd had sex. Looking back, I can see why.'

How to deal with sexual pressure

- Let your partner know what you feel comfortable with. This can change as your relationship changes. You may feel you become ready to try different things with your partner. Alternatively, you may decide you no longer want to give your consent for particular sexual activities. Have an open discussion about how you both feel. If your relationship is strong enough then you should be able to work things out.

- If the person is someone you have just met or have been going out with only for a short time, then be clear if you do not want to consent to something. Speak firmly but calmly and say something like, 'I'm not ready' or, 'I don't want to take things further'.

DISCUSS

1. Talk about how teenagers may feel pressurised to have sex.

   - Where might this pressure come from?

   - Is there more pressure on girls to have sex than there is on boys?

   - Who do you think is more likely to put pressure on their partner – a boy or a girl?

2. What would you say to a friend who is seeing someone who is putting pressure on your friend to have sex?

3.3 Having sex – teenagers' experiences

People have very different experiences the first time they have sex.

The first time

A 2019 study of young people between the ages of 17 and 24 suggested that 52 per cent of young women and 44 per cent of young men felt they were not ready when they lost their virginity.

For some people, the first time they have sex is everything they hoped it would be. For many it's exciting. They feel they have crossed a line and they enjoyed it. For others it doesn't quite live up to expectations, or they may wish that they had waited until they were with someone who listened to them and understood their feelings.

If you and your partner decide that you want to begin exploring sex together, then talk about what contraception and protection against STIs you are going to use. Make it clear to your partner that what you are doing is something private between the two of you and that you do not expect them to talk to their friends about it.

Many teenagers worry about what will happen the first time. They may be nervous about whether it will hurt or whether they will bleed. Or they may be nervous about how they look, whether they will know what to do, and whether their partner will enjoy it. Talking about what you plan to do, taking your time and sharing your feelings can help to make it a positive experience for both of you.

Teenagers talk about their first experiences of sex

'You imagine that the first time is going to be all romantic, but it was like a scene from a comedy. Somehow, I got my bra tangled in his belt and he fell over. Then we had to try three times to put the condom on. Just as we were getting started, we heard a noise at the front door, but it was just the post arriving. He started to giggle, but then pulled me back onto the bed and we did it. It was just as much fun as I'd hoped.' **Sadie**

'We didn't discuss contraception in detail because he said he'd look after it. But we didn't use a condom because we got carried away and I spent an awful time worrying until my period came. He wasn't that bothered and I realised that he didn't care about me as much as he should have.' **Magda**

'I was a bit embarrassed because I'd never been with a guy before and I wasn't sure what to do. But we talked about it and Patrick reassured me. We took our time, finding out what felt good for both of us. It was so amazing to finally be with someone who liked me as much as I liked him, and not to have to hide my feelings.' **Sam**

'We were both really nervous and excited. No one else was in the house. I lay down on the bed with Sonya and we slowly got undressed. We got under the duvet. It was very gentle and we both enjoyed it.' **Emily**

'I'd seen TV dramas and films showing sex scenes, and had thought that's what sex would be like in real life. It wasn't! I'm not saying it was better or worse, just different.' **Stefan**

DISCUSS

Discuss what these teenagers had to say about their first experiences of sex. What different types of experience did they have? What made some experiences more positive and others more negative?

Ask Erica

Dear Erica

My boyfriend wants to sleep with me, but I'm not sure about going the whole way. What should I do?

Nadia

WRITE

Write Erica's reply.

Kristen's story

Kristen's friends bragged about having had sex. She felt left out. She thought she was the only one who hadn't.

'I was only 14, but they kept on at me about why I hadn't had sex. They made me feel I wasn't as grown up as them.'

Shortly after, she agreed to have sex with her boyfriend Carl while her parents were out at work one day.

'We had sex on the bathroom floor because it was the only room with a lock,' she says. 'It all felt so sleazy that I regretted it immediately.'

She felt even worse when Carl was cold towards her as soon as they'd had sex, leaving the house soon afterwards.

Things got worse when Kristen confided to her friends that she had had sex with Carl, only to find that they had been lying and hadn't had sex themselves.

'Then Carl denied that we had had sex,' she says. 'His friends were teasing him and I think he was embarrassed about what had happened, which hurt. For months I dreaded going to school. I hated seeing Carl and worried what everyone thought about me.'

Kirsten was very upset but felt unable to confide in her parents because she was worried that they would be furious with her.

DISCUSS

1. Discuss Kristen's experience. Should she have realised her friends were lying? Why do people sometimes claim to have had sex when they haven't?

2. Discuss Carl's behaviour. Why do you think he left so quickly? What might he have been feeling? What do you think of the way he behaved?

3. Talk about how Carl's and Kristen's friends behaved. Why do you think Kristen and Carl were so worried about what other people thought?

4.1 STIs

When you have sex, no method of protection is 100% safe. That's why people call protecting yourself against sexually transmitted infections (STIs) 'safer sex' rather than 'safe sex'.

STIs: your questions answered

Q. What is an STI?

A. An STI is a sexually transmitted infection – an infection that is passed between people through sexual contact or skin-to-skin contact.

Q. What different types of STI are there?

A. You can get a number of different STIs. Some are caused by bacteria and can therefore be treated with antibiotics (for example, gonorrhoea, syphilis and chlamydia). Some are viruses (herpes, genital warts and HIV). Others are parasites (pubic lice).

Q. How do you know if you have an STI?

A. You may notice symptoms, such as a burning sensation when you pass urine, or an unusual discharge. Other STIs may have no symptoms or symptoms may not develop until weeks, months or even years later. The only way you can tell is to get yourself tested.

Q. Where do I get myself tested?

A. You can get yourself tested at a sexual health clinic or at a GP's surgery.

Q. Can STIs be cured?

A. Some can and some, such as HIV, can't. But they can all be treated and the earlier they are identified, the better. (Even though HIV cannot be cured, it can be controlled through daily use of the drug ART so that the infection cannot be passed on to sexual partners.)

Q. What are dental dams and when should you use them?

A. A dental dam is a thin, flexible, square piece of latex that can help to prevent the spread of STIs during oral sex. Dental dams are easy to use. You place one over your or your partner's vulva and/or anus so that it creates a barrier between the mouth and genitals.

Q. Does a condom protect you against catching an STI?

A. Using a condom reduces the chances of you getting an STI such as chlamydia, gonorrhoea or HIV. But condoms do not provide complete protection against infections that are passed on by skin-to-skin contact such as herpes, genital warts and syphilis.

Q. Is there anything that will give you complete protection against STIs?

A. The only thing that can give you complete protection is to avoid any sexual contact – but this is unrealistic for most people!

Protecting yourself against STIs

1. Use a condom and/or a dental dam. Some people make the mistake of thinking that if you have oral or anal sex you don't need to use a condom, because condoms are only necessary to prevent you from getting pregnant or passing on STIs through vaginal sex. Whatever type of sex you are having, using a condom and/or a dental dam offers protection against chlamydia and other STIs.

2. Get yourself checked for STIs regularly by going to a sexual health clinic or seeing your GP. Young people aged under 25 are advised to get checked once a year as a precaution.

3. If you have several partners, you stand more chance of getting an STI. So, if you change partners, it is worth both of you getting checked. As chlamydia and some other STIs have no symptoms you may not know you have an infection.

4. Talk to your partner about the risks of STIs, the benefits of regular check-ups, signs you should look out for and the need to use condoms or dental dams, even when you are enjoying non-penetrative sex.

Ask Erica

Dear Erica

I've been having sex with my boyfriend for a couple of months. We've been using condoms but he tells me he hates them and none of his friends use them. He says it'll be all right because he'll withdraw before he ejaculates, so I won't get pregnant and I won't catch anything because he knows he doesn't have any infections because he hasn't got any symptoms. What should I do?

Penny

WRITE

Write Erica's reply to Penny.

Chlamydia: a 'silent' STI

Chlamydia is a very common STI affecting thousands of young people in the UK. It is very easy to treat and cure, but it is difficult to diagnose without a test, because in many cases it has no symptoms.

If it is left untreated, it can cause pelvic inflammatory disease (PID). PID can cause permanent damage to the female reproductive system, making it harder or impossible for a woman to have children. It can infect the cervix and urinary tract, causing pelvic inflammatory disease if it reaches the fallopian tubes. In boys/men, it can infect the urinary tract and inflame or cause the testicles to swell, and can also cause infertility.

Chlamydia is spread through having vaginal, oral or anal sex with an infected person.

Approximately 80% of girls/women and 50% of boys/men who have the infection have no symptoms.

In boys/men, the symptoms can include:

- painful and swollen testicles
- burning or stinging when urinating
- pain or bleeding from the anus (if the person has had anal sex).

Symptoms in girls/women can include:

- pain when having sex
- burning or stinging when urinating
- bleeding between periods
- a yellowish discharge from the vagina.

These symptoms can take weeks to appear and often do not appear at all.

It is possible to catch chlamydia again even after you have been successfully treated for it, if you have unprotected sex with someone who is infected.

Chlamydia can be diagnosed through a urine sample for boys/men or by taking a swab from the vagina for girls/women. It can be cured by a course of antibiotics.

Chlamydia tests can be carried out at a sexual health clinic, GP surgery or at some pharmacies. Self-testing kits are also available on the NHS.

Jayden's story

'I had oral sex with this girl I met at a party. I didn't think we needed to use a condom because it wasn't as if we were having full sex.

'A few days later I got flu-like symptoms and a burning sensation when I urinated. I thought it was a urine infection so I went to the doctor. She asked me to give a urine sample and sent it off to be tested.

'I was shocked when it came back saying I'd got chlamydia. The doctor said I was lucky because lots of people with chlamydia have no symptoms. She gave me a course of strong antibiotics and advice on practising safer sex.'

RESEARCH

Visit the Brook and Sexwise websites to find out more about chlamydia. How common is this STI?

4.2 Symptoms of STIs

It can be difficult to know if you have an STI because there may be no symptoms initially.

This means that a person who is infected can unknowingly infect other people, so it is important to have yourself tested, particularly if you have had unprotected sex.

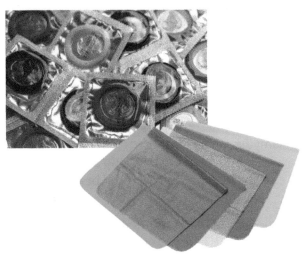

The best way to protect yourself against STIs is to use a condom or dental dam during oral, vaginal or anal sex.

Gonorrhoea

The symptoms of gonorrhoea appear in a boy/man between about two and ten days after he becomes infected. Gonorrhoea can cause pain when urinating and a yellowish discharge from the penis.

In a girl/woman the gonorrhoea bacteria can cause inflammation of the opening of the womb, but this is not usually painful. Gonorrhoea can cause pain on passing urine and vaginal discharge, and sometimes pain in the abdomen or pelvis. But in the early stages there are no obvious symptoms.

The best way to protect against gonorrhoea is to have protected sex.

Syphilis

Syphilis is one of the STIs with which you can be infected without having any symptoms. Between ten days and twelve weeks after infection a painless sore, called a chancre, can appear on or near the sex organs. It can clearly be seen if it develops on the penis, but if it is inside the vagina or anus the person may know nothing about it.

Within a few days the sore will clear up on its own. But this doesn't mean that the person is cured. Unless they get treatment, the infection will spread to other parts of the body. A few weeks later the disease will enter its second stage, and can cause various symptoms, such as skin rashes, mouth sores, fever, a sore throat and a general feeling of ill-health. In time these symptoms will also disappear.

The disease then enters the third stage, during which the bacteria continue to attack the body, but there are no apparent symptoms. The third stage can last for many years. Eventually, however, syphilis can affect the nervous system or the cardiovascular system, causing strokes, heart problems, meningitis, dementia symptoms, loss of coordination and blindness.

Again, the best way to protect against syphilis and the other infections discussed here is to use a condom and/or dental dam and for you and your partner(s) to have regular STI tests.

HIV

HIV or the Human Immunodeficiency Virus is one of the most serious STIs. It damages the cells in the immune system, weakening the body's ability to fight everyday infections and disease. If the virus is not diagnosed and treated, it can lead to your immune system being severely damaged and to the life-threatening illnesses caused by AIDS (acquired immune deficiency syndrome).

Today antiretroviral treatment can stop most people with HIV developing AIDS, if they are tested and treated early enough.

How can you be infected?

HIV can be transmitted if an infected person's bodily fluids (blood, semen or vaginal fluids) enter another person's body. Infection most commonly happens through vaginal or anal sex without a condom. It can also be passed on by sharing needles or from mother to child during pregnancy, birth or breastfeeding.

How can't you be infected?

You can't catch HIV by shaking hands, kissing, hugging or sharing cutlery, towels or toilet seats with an infected person. Urine, sweat and saliva do not contain enough of the HIV virus for this to happen.

How can you tell if you have been infected?

You can be tested for HIV four weeks after you have been infected. The test is available for free at sexual health clinics and some GP surgeries. If you think you have been exposed to HIV, it is possible to be prescribed a treatment called PEP from a sexual health clinic or HIV clinic to try to stop an infection developing. It must be taken as soon as possible, within 72 hours of having sex.

Genital warts

Genital warts are small fleshy growths on the genitals or anus. If they are inside the vagina, on the cervix or in the anus you may not know they are there. Genital warts are caused by a strain of the human papillomavirus (HPV) which can be prevented by having the HPV vaccine. This is now available to all Year 8 students at school in England, Wales and Northern Ireland, as some high-risk strains of the HPV virus can cause a range of cancers. Ninety per cent of people infected with HPV do not develop warts and so they can pass on the infection without realising it.

Genital warts are not a serious threat to your overall health. However, they can be uncomfortable and may itch. They can be treated by your doctor or a sexual health clinic with special creams or cryotherapy – 'freezing therapy'. (Do not use wart creams that you can buy over the counter, as they are not suitable for the moist tissues around the genitals.)

Genital herpes

Genital herpes is caused by the herpes simplex virus, which also causes cold sores. It produces blisters in the genital area which burst and form ulcers. They are caught by skin-to-skin contact. There is therefore a risk of getting genital herpes from someone who has cold sores when having oral sex. If they are not treated, the sores will disappear after two to three weeks, but the virus remains in the body for life and they may reoccur.

Pubic lice

Pubic lice are tiny insects that live in a person's pubic hair. They cause itching and irritation of the genital area. They are commonly referred to as crabs. They are not a threat to a person's general health.

DISCUSS

- Which STI do you think is most misunderstood by young people?
- Which one are young people least aware of?

Give reasons for your views.

Ask Erica

Dear Erica

I had unprotected sex and am worried I may have caught an STI. How can I tell?

Worried, Belfast

WRITE

Write Erica's reply to Worried.

DISCUSS

1. Which do you think are the most serious STIs?
2. What precautions can you take?

Give reasons for your views.

WRITE

In groups, imagine that you have been asked to plan a video giving information about STIs as part of a campaign to make people of your own age aware of the importance of practising safer sex. Create a storyboard giving details of what each part of the video would contain.

4.3 Sexual health clinics

If you think you may be at risk of having an STI, you can get yourself tested at a sexual health clinic. You can find information about your nearest clinic online.

Sexual health clinics: your questions answered

Q. Do I need to make an appointment?

A. At many clinics you do not need an appointment. But you may have to wait for a considerable time if they are busy.

Q. Do I need to prepare for the visit in any way?

A. You may be asked to give a urine sample, so it's a good idea not to urinate for two hours before the visit.

Q. What happens when I arrive?

A. Go to reception and register. They will ask your name and why you have come. You can give a false name if you wish.

Q. Who will see me?

A. You'll be seen by a specialist doctor or nurse who will ask you some questions such as: Why are you concerned? What symptoms do you have? Who have you been having sex with? What type of sex did you have – vaginal, oral or anal?

Q. Will they examine me?

A. They may need to check your genitals for any sign of infection.

Q. Will I have to give any samples?

A. Depending on your symptoms and the type of sex you have been having, you may be asked to give a urine sample or a blood sample, and you may need to have a swab from your vagina, penis, anus or throat.

Q. How long will I have to wait for the results of any tests?

A. Some results may be available that day. Other samples may have to be tested in a laboratory and you may have to wait for several days for the results.

Q. How will I get the results?

A. The doctor or nurse will discuss with you how you will receive the results. Normally they will be sent by text message, or the clinic may ring you.

Q. Will I have to go to the clinic again?

A. That depends on whether you need treatment.

Q. If I'm under 16, will they tell my parents, my doctor or my school?

A. No, they won't tell anyone about your visit or any treatment you require. The conversations you have and the treatment you receive are confidential (unless the clinic has any concerns about your safety).

How to deal with an STI

- If you think you may have an STI, stop having sex with anyone until you have had a medical check.

- Get yourself tested at a local clinic. At many clinics you don't need to make an appointment.

- If you have an STI, tell anyone you've had sex with, so that they can be treated too.

- Avoid unprotected sex in the future and make sure you have regular STI screenings.

Screening for STIs

Public Health England recommends that anyone under 25 who is sexually active should be tested annually for chlamydia and whenever they change partners.

Boys who have sex with boys are recommended to have annual tests and to be tested every three months if they have unprotected sex or sex with several partners.

DISCUSS

1. Which do you think are the most useful pieces of advice?

2. Does any of the advice surprise you?

Give reasons for your views.

Half of young people do not use condoms for sex with new partner

By Tom Barnes

About half of young people will not use a condom the first time they have sex with a new partner, according to new research.

A YouGov study of more than 2000 16–24-year-olds found 47 percent who were sexually active did not use protection when sleeping with someone new.

One in ten of those surveyed said they had never used a condom.

A third of young adults taking part in the survey said that they had never seen a condom mentioned in sex scenes on TV and in films.

The poll was carried out as part of a Public Health England (PHE) campaign aimed at reducing rates of sexually transmitted infections (STIs) among young people.

There were over 140,000 diagnoses of chlamydia and gonorrhoea in people aged 15–24 in England in 2016, according to government statistics.

The Independent, 15 December 2017

DISCUSS

Study the article and discuss the following questions.

1. Why do you think so many 16–24-year-olds do not use condoms?

2. Why do you think condoms aren't mentioned in sex scenes on TV and in films?

3. Should TV programmes and films have to extend the warnings at the start about scenes of a sexual nature to include a warning that the sex scenes do not mention condoms?

The C-Card scheme

confidential, conversation, choice

A C-Card from the Sunderland scheme

As a young person, you can join something called the 'C-Card scheme'. Once you register with the scheme, you will be assessed, shown how to use a condom and given a card (similar to a credit card). You can then pick up free condoms from local distribution points. Your local scheme may also offer things like free lubricant, dental dams, femidoms and screening kits for chlamydia and gonorrhoea. The aims of the scheme are to encourage condom use and to promote good sexual health by introducing young people to clinics and services in their area. Your local scheme may ask you to visit a registration point after a set period of time so your sexual health needs can be reviewed.

DISCUSS

1. Were you aware of the C-Card scheme before you read about it in this book?

2. Do you think schools should do more to raise awareness of the scheme? Give reasons for your views.

5.1 Child abuse

Child abuse is when a child is hurt or harmed by the behaviour of an adult.

Types of child abuse

There are several types of child abuse.

- **Physical abuse** – This is when an adult hits, punches or kicks a child, or deliberately hurts them physically in some other way.
- **Emotional abuse** – This involves treatment which seriously affects emotional development, such as withholding affection, ignoring a child, bullying or being excessively strict.
- **Verbal abuse** – This is constantly being sarcastic, shouting, making derogatory remarks and posting cruel messages online.
- **Sexual abuse** – This is when children are made to take part in sexual activities, including grooming them (*see Unit 5.2*) or encouraging them to watch sex acts online.
- **Neglect** – This is not looking after a child properly by making sure that they have enough to eat, have clothes to wear and living conditions where they can stay healthy.

Physical abuse

In the past, some people believed that the best way to punish children who misbehaved was to inflict a physical punishment, which would act as a deterrent to stop them misbehaving in the future. This is illegal today, although in a court of law parents in England can defend smacking their child if their actions are seen as a 'reasonable punishment'. The law has been changed in Scotland and Wales to remove this defence.

DISCUSS

1. Discuss the views expressed below.

'A good smack never did anybody any harm and it taught children right from wrong.'

'It is a child's right not to be physically punished in any way.'

Facts about abuse

Here are some true and false statements about sexual and physical abuse.

a) Girls are more at risk than boys.

FALSE: Boys are at risk as much as girls, though they are less likely to report it.

b) Children with disabilities are three times more likely to be abused than those without disabilities.

TRUE: Children with physical and mental disabilities are more vulnerable than other children.

c) In nine out of ten instances of child abuse that are reported, the offender was a relative or someone known by the child.

TRUE: It is a myth that most offences are committed by strangers.

d) The majority of people who are guilty of offences of abuse are men.

TRUE: However, there are a number of women who are responsible for abusing children.

e) In the majority of cases of physical abuse of teenagers, the person is abused by their boyfriend or girlfriend.

TRUE: This is often because they will not do what the other person wants.

f) In 2017 over 50 000 children were identified as needing protection.

TRUE: The actual number was 58 000.

g) Many cases of sexual abuse go unreported.

TRUE: There are many reasons for this. The victim may be too frightened or too ashamed to tell anyone.

h) Victims are sometimes to blame for the abuse because of the way they have behaved.

FALSE: It is never the victim's fault, no matter how they have behaved. It is always the abuser's fault.

i) It is sexual abuse to make a child watch pornography.

TRUE: A person who makes you do things you do not want to do is abusing you even if there is no physical contact.

j) Victims of abuse should always tell someone about it.

TRUE: Even if the abuser is a close family member, it is important to tell someone else about it.

Help and support

When you have told an adult about being abused, they may have to involve other adults to help get things sorted out. You may have to talk to a social worker and a police officer. You may have to be examined by a doctor.

An investigation will be carried out. During the investigation, you may be asked some questions which you find embarrassing or difficult, but the adults will be used to dealing with cases of abuse and will make it as easy as possible for you to say what happened.

They may then hold a case conference to decide what action to take. If it is decided to prosecute the offender, you may have to give evidence in court. Your evidence may be given by video link so that you do not have to come face to face with your abuser.

Every effort will be made to help prevent you from getting upset and there will be an adult there to support you at each stage.

DISCUSS

In pairs, study the true and false statements about sexual and physical abuse.

- Do any of the facts surprise you?
- What did you learn about child abuse from reading the answers?

Sexual abuse – it's important to tell someone

Elena Taylor explains why.

It's vital for someone who is being sexually abused to tell an adult about it. It's important to tell someone in order to stop the abuse. The longer it goes on, the more damaging it is likely to be.

It can be difficult because the adult responsible may be a relative or family friend. But it is a crime and the consequences of not telling may have long-lasting effects. Anyone who has been abused may find it hard to trust people and to form relationships. They may find it hard to concentrate and their school work may suffer. They may have low self-esteem and suffer from depression. The sooner a person speaks up, the sooner they will get the help they need.

RESEARCH

Visit the NSPCC (National Society for the Prevention of Cruelty to Children) and Childline websites to find out more about child abuse and the advice given to anyone experiencing it.

Fact check

Under 19s worried about any kind of abuse can talk in confidence to an advisor at Childline, either by calling the helpline for free on 0800 1111 or visiting the website www.childline.org.uk. The helpline is open 24/7.

DISCUSS

1. According to Elena Taylor, why is it important to tell someone about sexual abuse?
2. What effects does being abused have on the lives of victims?

5.2 Grooming

Grooming is when a person builds up an emotional connection with a young person in order to abuse them or sexually exploit them.

The person may be a stranger or someone you know such as a relative or a family friend. They could be any age and could be male or female. Grooming may take place online or face to face.

Fact check

In 2017, a new law was introduced making sexual communication with a child a criminal offence. A person found guilty of grooming can be given a two-year prison sentence and is automatically put on the sex offenders register.

The tricks that are used to groom you

Be internet wise. Be aware of the tactics that predators use to groom you online.

- They'll ask you to go private. They'll tell you that they think you are special and you can chat about things more freely if there's only the two of you and no one else is able to see or hear what you are saying.

- They'll try to find out as much as they can about what your interests are. What music do you like? What's your favourite band? What films and TV programmes do you like? Then they can use this information to say they share your interests and to offer to get you gifts like concert tickets.

- They'll appear to be sympathetic to try to get you to confide in them.

- They'll use flattery. They may suggest that a good-looking person like you could be a model. They may suggest that they know someone they could introduce you to.

- They may tempt you with money. They'll say things like, 'Let me have some photos and I'll see what I can get for them.'

- They may use intimidation and threaten to send pictures that you've sent them to your parents or their friends unless you do what they want.

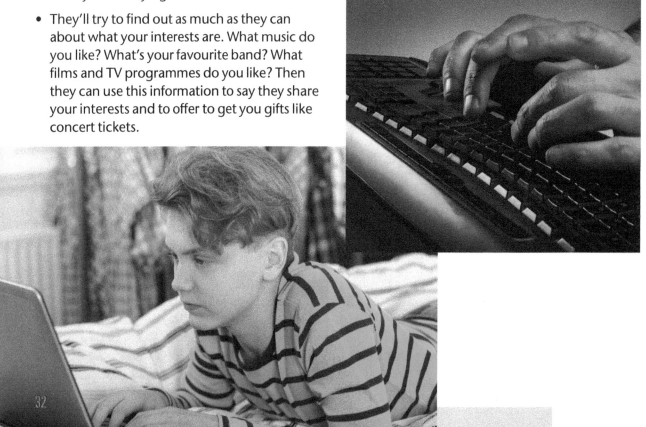

Mared's Story

'At 14, I was excited to get male attention.'

Mared Parry was 14 when she started to use social media. She had never received male attention before, but online she found that older men – in their mid-20s – started sending her messages.

'They began innocent and 14-year-old me was excited,' she recalls. 'To have an older guy call me beautiful made me feel special. In a sense I felt validated, or that I was actually worth something after all and wasn't ugly like the guys my age made me feel.'

When the messages turned sexual, the Cardiff University graduate, now 21, played along for the most part, and although she never met with them, she sent the men semi-nude pictures.

'It makes me sick thinking those images still exist, and that they were able to take advantage of me so easily,' she says. 'I didn't recognise it as grooming – it felt so innocent and normal.'

The Daily Telegraph, 11 June 2018

Scenario

You are 15 and you've never had a real boyfriend. You make friends in a chatroom with someone who says he's your age. You get along with him really well online. He says he's never been able to talk to anyone about his feelings before. He makes you feel special, so when he says he'd like to meet up, you agree but take a friend with you. It's only when you meet him that you realise that he's much older and that you've been tricked.

Case study – Rotherham

In 2012, it was revealed that a major case of child sexual exploitation had been taking place in the town of Rotherham. This had involved face-to-face grooming of children from the mid-1990s until at least 2007. Over 20 men have now been prosecuted for their part in the events and further trials are still to happen.

It is estimated there were at least 1500 victims, mostly girls between the ages of 11 and 18.

The men used techniques similar to those used to groom children and young people online. First, the men would try to get the children's attention. They would befriend them, flattering them to build up a relationship. They would buy them gifts, including food and alcohol.

Eventually, the men would invite them to come somewhere with them, such as a party. Then, at the party or in a lonely area, they would sexually assault their victims.

Often, the victims chosen were the most vulnerable people in society, such as looked-after children. These children may have been less likely to tell the authorities about what had happened – and in many cases when they did, they were not believed or taken seriously. The case has led to a major review of children's services, the police and the local council to make sure this can never happen again.

DISCUSS

1. Discuss the scenario. What steps could a young person take to protect themselves in this situation?

   Share your views in groups, then in a class discussion.

2. How can you tell whether a person you meet online is telling the truth about their age and gender?

3. What should you do if you think someone is grooming you?

Remember, anyone who is the victim of grooming should not feel guilty. It is not their fault. It is always the predator who is to blame.

RESEARCH

Visit the Childline, NSPCC and CEOP (Child Exploitation Online Protection) websites to find out what support is available to young people who have been abused or are worried they are being groomed.

WRITE

Design a poster warning young people of the dangers of accepting gifts and getting into relationships with older people. Include on the poster what you found out in your research and details of where people can go for help.

5.3 Sexting — it's no laughing matter

Sharing images of yourself or someone else naked or semi-naked is against the law and can end up being very embarrassing. You need to think carefully about what could happen.

Fact check

Remember: taking, possessing or sharing naked or sexual photos of someone under 18 is illegal. The maximum sentence for possessing an indecent image of a child is five years' imprisonment. For distributing indecent images of children, the maximum sentence is ten years in prison.

Think before you click

Before you share an image of yourself or someone else, think about the consequences. What could happen to that image in the future?

Questions to ask yourself before you send someone naked or sexual images:

- What does the law say about taking, sharing and owning naked pictures of people under 18?
- Why does the other person want me to do this?
- What if I refuse? Will they accept that I have a right to refuse?
- Am I thinking clearly about this request? Am I a bit flattered that they want to see me naked?
- Can I trust them not to show the pictures to anyone else?
- What would the consequences be if the pictures were to be sent to my parents or to everyone at school?
- If I agree, how will I feel about it in the future if the pictures are still out there?
- What if I fall out with this person in the future? Could I trust them with the images then?

Questions to ask yourself before you ask a someone to send you naked or sexual images:

- How would I feel if someone asked for naked pictures of me?
- What would my parents think if they knew what I was doing?
- What does the law say about owning naked pictures of under 18s?

Amy's story

'I went to this party one Saturday evening and everyone was drinking. This boy I knew was messing about with his mates. He pulled up my top and started touching me. One of his mates was filming us. They were laughing and saying horrible things. They only stopped when an older girl came in and told them to leave me alone.

'Next day there were messages and pictures online showing the boy groping me. And when I went to school I felt awful because everyone had seen them.'

YOUR CHOICE

Read Amy's story and then study the comments below.

1. Which are statements of fact and which are opinions?

2. Which of the opinions do you agree or disagree with? Give your reasons.

   'The boys should be ashamed.'

   'The boy who filmed her was committing a criminal offence.'

   'Sharing Amy's pictures without her consent is a crime.'

   'Amy will put it in perspective eventually and realise that it is no big deal.'

   'Amy had a narrow escape.'

   'The boy who groped her should be put on the sex offenders register.'

   'Amy will never be able to forget the incident.'

Ask Erica

Dear Erica

My girlfriend says she's curious to know what boys do when they are alone in their rooms. She says she wants some pictures and that she'll keep them to herself. I'm thinking there's no harm in it. Should I just send her some pics?

Harvey

WRITE

Write Erica's reply to Harvey. Look at the questions above to guide your answer.

Sharing revealing photos and videos of yourself online

The consequences of sharing photos or videos of yourself with someone you don't know can be much more serious.

The scenarios and advice that follow are from the *TES Online Safety Special Edition* (13 October 2017).

Scenario 1

You are 15 years old and a boy in your year says you are pretty. He says he likes you. He asks you to send him a topless photo of yourself. You do it, because everyone does it, don't they? It's just a laugh. Just one click. And then he says he is going to send the image to your friends or parents, unless …

Scenario 2

You're on a social media platform, in a chatroom or playing games online. A message pops up from what appears to be a teenage girl or boy, saying that you look great and they want to see more of you. Can you send them a picture? They'll send you some pictures back.

You don't know them, but this is normal, right? You send it. It's just a bit of fun. You send more, and then they ask for videos and you send those too. Finally, they ask you to go to a live streaming site, where they can see you, but you can't see them.

Scenario 3

You are 15 years old and someone contacts you to say that they are a modelling agent. They tell you that you could be a model. They ask you to send them some pictures of you looking glamorous, for example in a swimsuit. And you agree. It can't do any harm.

Then they tell you you need to look sexy and they encourage you to take your clothes off. You don't want them to think you're uptight. So you agree.

The money they are promising is great. So you agree to video yourself. You're safe in your room. It's harmless. You don't think about who else might see the video or what they might do with it.

What happens next?

If you're lucky, your parents might spot the messages and report them to the police. When the sexual exploitation team (SET) intervenes, they say that children in this situation are usually embarrassed, but they often don't realise the seriousness of the situation.

'Because it's not physical, because it's all online, it is not real to them,' says Danielle Power, a detective with the SET team. 'They just do not see the danger.'

She says she has dealt with many cases in which the victim even says they think the situation is funny.

If the activity does not come to the attention of the police, it can go one of two ways. The offender (who usually isn't who they are pretending to be) may threaten to send the pictures to your friends and family unless you do x or y. Alternatively, because they just want the images, they may keep asking for more.

Remember: if you are concerned about messages or conversations you are having with anyone online you can contact Childline, CEOP (the Child Exploitation and Online Protection centre) or the police.

ROLE PLAY

In pairs, role play a friend talking to the young person involved in each of the scenarios. What would you say to try to convince them not to send the photographs and videos?

6.1 What is stereotyping?

Stereotyping means believing that people from one group all share the same characteristics.

Stereotypes can be based on very general categories, such as ethnicity or nationality ('Jamaican people like reggae'), gender ('women are bad drivers'), age ('old people are intolerant') or sexuality ('lesbians are butch'). They can also be quite specific, such as 'blind people have good hearing' or 'you can't trust politicians'.

Stereotyping is a lazy and dangerous way of labelling people.

- Stereotypes are inaccurate. They are simplified and distorted images based on incomplete knowledge, half-truths and falsehoods. They therefore give us a false picture of society.

- Stereotypes reinforce prejudice and discrimination. They make it easier for groups to become the victims of prejudice. For example, if you believe that older people are intolerant, it makes it easier to dismiss them and their views.

- Stereotyping stops us from seeing people as individuals. Everyone is unique and should not be labelled simply as belonging to a group and behaving in a particular way.

- All stereotypes are negative. Take a statement that might seem positive, such as 'Black people are good at sport'. This stereotypical belief could have very negative consequences, by limiting the opportunities made available to a group of young people.

DISCUSS

On your own, study the following statements and pick out those that are based on stereotypes. Then discuss your answers in groups.

> Goalkeepers are often over six feet tall.
> People who wear glasses are unattractive.
> Tennis players have good hand–eye coordination.
> Politicians do not tell the truth.
> All girls want to be princesses.
> People who are left-handed are clumsy.
> People with pale skin get sunburnt more easily.
> Jockeys are lightweight and small.
> Teenagers are only interested in themselves.
> Welsh people are more musical than other groups.
> People who are unemployed are workshy.

YOUR CHOICE

1. Study the list of words below. Which of them do you associate with men and which with women?

- muscled
- weak
- attractive
- beautiful
- aggressive
- stubborn
- imaginative
- emotional
- wealthy
- caring
- handsome
- sensitive
- sporting
- artistic
- rich
- slim
- powerful
- passionate
- strong
- practical

2. Draw a table like the one below and then put each of the words in the appropriate column.

Men	Women	Both men and women

Discuss your lists with other members of the class. Do your lists vary according to your gender?

3. What does this exercise reveal about stereotyping?

DISCUSS

Talk about what you have learned about stereotyping.

1. Have you or anyone you know ever been stereotyped? What did it feel like to be stereotyped?

2. Have you ever stereotyped anyone, then had to change your mind about them when you got to know them better ?

Media stereotyping

The media can reinforce stereotypes by the way they present groups. They influence opinions and attitudes. For example, the media often sensationalise news stories about young people, suggesting that teenagers are violent troublemakers who hang around being loud and abusive. The stereotypical teenager is dressed in a hoodie and is reckless, foul mouthed and lazy.

Some teenagers might behave like this, but the majority do not. To suggest that all teenagers behave badly is to present a stereotypical view of young people.

What teenagers say about being stereotyped

No one likes to be stereotyped. These teenagers explain how stereotyping presents a distorted view of teenagers.

Nassam Ocheby is doing his A levels and plans to go to medical school to become a doctor. He likes to play badminton and has been learning to play the piano. He is the complete opposite of the stereotypical teenager presented by the media.

Fay Holland, from Lancashire, says, 'The news reports contradict each other. According to some papers, all 16-year-old girls are running around getting pregnant, but the average age of a first-time mother is now above 30. And what about our academic successes? Apparently, they can be explained away by easier exams. I know many teenagers who are amazingly positive people and do amazingly positive things. A whole generation can't be inherently bad.'

Dein Harry, from London, says, 'People need to stop believing everything they see or read and make their own judgements based on personal experiences. It's time for adults to do some growing up.'

Henry's story

Henry Katende is a refugee from Uganda, who now lives in London. This is his story.

'Recently I found myself in an intimidating situation in the middle of the day. One minute I was just someone in a rush, late for an appointment, and the next I was pulled off the street by a police officer and questioned about the way I was dressed. Knowing that my attitude could make the difference between arrest and freedom, I politely answered his questions.

'This interrogation left me questioning what has gone wrong in our society. Young people have been labelled as being a danger to society and are treated accordingly. The small minority who behave antisocially shouldn't influence the way most young people are viewed.'

DISCUSS

1. Discuss Dein's and Fay's views. Do you agree with Dein that people's views should be based on personal experiences rather than on what they see or read?

2. Talk about Henry Katende's experience. How would you have felt if you were Henry? What do you learn from his experience about the consequences of stereotyping?

3. Do you agree that the media present a stereotypical picture of teenagers? Can you provide any evidence to support your views?

RESEARCH IT

In groups, draw up a list of different groups, such as young men or women, ethnic minorities or religious groups that are often stereotyped in the media – in newspapers and magazines and/or in films and TV programmes.

Print out any examples of stereotyping you find and together produce a wall chart consisting of the pictures and stories you have found, and what you think about these examples of stereotyping.

6.2 What is prejudice?

Prejudice literally means 'prejudging someone', that is, making a judgement about them (usually negative) based on little or no knowledge. Having stereotyped views about certain groups automatically leads to prejudice.

People's prejudices can be based on many different things such as ethnicity, gender, religion, disability or age. Many prejudices are based on anxieties and fears about other people being different from themselves.

Are you prejudiced?

Most people like to think they treat other people fairly. However, often we treat people according to opinions that we already hold. Our first impression of someone is based on their appearance. We might see someone sleeping rough and wonder if they are a drug addict, when in fact they are an ex-serviceman suffering from post-traumatic stress disorder. Or we may see a burly shaven-headed man walking straight towards us and step aside to let them pass because we think that people who shave their heads are more likely to start a fight.

How can you tell what a person is like?

YOUR CHOICE

On your own, study each statement and decide whether you agree or disagree with it. Then compare your views in a class discussion.

You can tell what a person is like by:

- the clothes they wear
- the way they walk or move around
- listening to their accent
- how often they swear
- how they eat
- how they treat animals
- the area in which they live
- how much money they have
- what their manners are like
- the colour of their skin
- what their religion is
- how they behave towards other people
- the opinions they hold
- who their friends are
- whether they have any tattoos.

Groups

We often fit people into groups – male, female, young, old, straight or gay – and when we put people into groups, we expect members of that group to behave in a particular way. This can lead to prejudice. For example, lots of young people go to football matches to sing songs and support their club. To categorise them all as hooligans would be to stereotype them.

Belonging to groups

We like to surround ourselves with people who are similar to ourselves, because we feel more comfortable belonging to a group. A group can be your family, your neighbours, people of your own age, people you chat to online, your class at school,

the members of a sports club or a religious group. As individuals we are drawn towards people like ourselves and we may have a natural tendency to be prejudiced against people who are different from us.

WRITE

On your own, list all the groups you belong to. Write down any attitudes and values that one of these groups has. Do they have any prejudices against people who aren't in their group?

DISCUSS

Share your views in a class discussion.

Fact check

A hate crime is any criminal act based on prejudice or hostility to a person because of their race or ethnicity, sexual orientation, disability, religion, beliefs or transgender identity.

Three quarters of hate incidents recorded by the police are to do with race. They range from throwing rubbish into a garden and writing graffiti, hoax phone calls and abusive messages, offensive jokes and name calling to threats of violence, bullying and intimidation.

When a hate incident is a criminal offence it is a hate crime.

Bailey's story

13-year-old Bailey Anderson and his friend were walking down a street in North Belfast in May 2016 on their way to band practice. Two men attacked them because they were Protestants, calling them 'dirty wee prods'. Bailey had been pushed up against a wall and repeatedly punched in the face by the time some passers-by intervened and the violence stopped. Apart from the physical harm he suffered, Bailey was left feeling afraid for his safety when out in public and distressed that religious prejudice and violence is still happening today. 'I was scared and shocked. It made me feel annoyed that I can't go somewhere without being attacked because of my religion.'

Racism on Ryanair

In October 2018 a Ryanair passenger racially abused an elderly woman sitting next to him on a plane. Another passenger filmed the incident on his mobile phone and uploaded it to social media.

The man was filmed calling the 77-year-old victim an 'ugly black *********' and shouting 'don't talk to me in a foreign language you stupid ugly cow'.

Customers threatened to boycott the airline after its staff failed to remove him from the flight from Barcelona to London Stansted – leaving the elderly woman to move seats instead.

[The footage] shows the man shouting at the woman to move seats while her daughter tries to tell him her mother is disabled.

The man then swears at the woman again, and tells staff to move the woman to another seat, adding: 'If you don't go to another seat I'll push you to another seat.'

Staff can be heard telling him 'don't be so rude, you have to calm down' while other passengers call for the man to be thrown off the flight.

The Independent, 22 October 2018

DISCUSS

1. Discuss the following views. Which do you agree with and why?

    'The only way to change such behaviour is to challenge it.'

    'Being a bystander while a hate crime is committed is tantamount to condoning it.'

    'You must always intervene when you see a hate incident, whatever the circumstances.'

    'If you witness a hate crime, you must always report it, otherwise you are allowing the perpetrators to get away with it.'

    'You should only intervene in a hate incident if it's safe to do so.'

2. In groups, imagine you are witness to a racist incident, such as one of those described in this unit. What would you do? Why?

Discussion of prejudice against people with disabilities and older people can be found in Unit 16.

More details on hate crimes can be found in Your Choice: Book Three, *Unit 3.*

7.1 Recreational drugs

Pharmaceutical drugs are taken as medical treatments, such as antibiotics to combat infections and painkillers to manage pain. Illegal 'recreational drugs' are usually taken for the pleasant feelings they give the user, but they can have unpredictable effects and can be addictive.

Cannabis (hash, weed, dope, skunk)

Cannabis comes from the marijuana plant. It can be smoked, vaped or eaten. It is the most widely used illegal drug in the UK.

The effects of cannabis differ from person to person. Some people feel relaxed and happy, while others become confused and anxious, or may feel sleepy and lethargic. It can affect a person's memory.

Does cannabis have a medical use?

Cannabis oil can be used to treat epilepsy, to reduce nausea caused by chemotherapy and to reduce the pain of muscle spasms in multiple sclerosis. There is some evidence that it can help people with post-traumatic stress disorder.

Myth: cannabis is harmless

It is difficult to assess the long-term effects of cannabis, but it is likely to have similar effects to tobacco smoking, particularly if it is smoked with tobacco. The risks of lung, throat and mouth cancers are probably the same as for tobacco smokers. The risks increase according to the strength and amount of cannabis that is used.

About 10 per cent of regular users of cannabis become addicted to it.

Cannabis has also been linked to mental health problems, in particular with psychosis, causing individuals to lose touch with reality, hallucinating and seeing and hearing things that are not there. There is evidence that heavy use of cannabis as a teenager increases the risk of developing mental illnesses including depression and schizophrenia. This is becoming more of a problem as the strength of cannabis has increased, with varieties such as super skunk becoming more common.

A cannabis shop in Vancover, Canada.

Should cannabis be decriminalised or legalised?

Decriminalisation means that it would no longer be an offence to possess small amounts of cannabis for personal use.

Legalisation means that to grow and supply cannabis would no longer be illegal. You would be able to buy cannabis in shops, though the shops would be licensed and it would remain illegal to sell it to anyone under the age of 18.

People in favour of legalisation argue that cannabis is less harmful than alcohol, that it would stop criminals controlling the supply, that the police would not have to spend time dealing with cannabis and would be able to concentrate on more serious drug offences, and that the government would be able to tax suppliers and thus increase their income.

Opponents of legalisation argue that it would lead to more widespread use, that it is a dangerous drug to which regular users can become addicted and that its long-term effects are not yet known.

Canada has recently legalised cannabis, but there are still many restrictions on its use. Research what these restrictions are, and how some of the laws vary from province to province.

In groups, act out a scenario where a radio presenter on a chat show is having a discussion with three people about cannabis in the UK:

- one guest thinks the situation should stay as it is,
- one thinks it should be decriminalised,
- the third thinks it should be legalised.

MDMA (ecstasy)

MDMA or ecstasy is a synthetic drug that usually comes in the form of tablets.

MDMA tablets come in different shapes and sizes, often with a design or logo printed on them.

MDMA is popular with clubbers because it produces feelings of increased energy, pleasure and affection. It also affects perception, making sounds and colours more intense. The effects last for between three and six hours.

MDMA affects three chemicals in the brain: dopamine, which produces increased energy; norepinephrine, which increases the heart rate and blood pressure; and serotonin, which affects mood.

It also affects the body's temperature control system. If someone who has taken MDMA dances in a hot atmosphere for too long, they may become dehydrated and overheat. This can be dangerous, particularly if they drink too much water, because MDMA causes the body to release a hormone which stops it producing urine. Drinking too much too quickly can affect the balance of salt in the body, which can be as dangerous as not drinking enough water.

Short-term effects can include anxiety and panic attacks. No one can predict how an individual will react. There is some evidence to suggest that using MDMA contributes to damage to the liver and kidneys. It has also been linked to heart and memory problems.

The risks

If someone buys MDMA from a dealer, they do not know exactly what they are getting. Testers at the Boomtown Fair in 2018 found that 90% of the substances tested were drugs, but 10% contained other substances such as plaster of Paris, monosodium glutamate, creatine, sugar and anti-malarial pills. Users have no way of knowing how strong the MDMA is or how they will react to it.

Megan Bell, 17, who died at the T in the Park festival in 2016, had three times the lethal amount of the drug in her system when she died.

'There is no safe way of using ecstasy. There will always be a risk involved in taking this very dangerous drug,' advises psychiatrist Dr Prun Bijral.

'If you do take that risk, don't use alone. Make sure friends are around, so they can get immediate help from the emergency services if you start to feel ill.'

In pairs, make a list of at least five important things you have learned about MDMA from this page, then compare your lists in a class discussion.

Act out a scene in which two people argue about the risks of taking MDMA, with one saying it's worth the risk and the other saying it's not. Take it in turns to play each role.

Research the statistics about, and the rise and fall in death rates from MDMA over the past 30 years, and see if you can find out any reasons for these ups and downs.

7.2 New psychoactive substances

New psychoactive substances (NPS) produce similar effects to illegal drugs such as cannabis and LSD (see below). In the past they were often referred to as 'legal highs' because it was possible to buy them legally at festivals and in headshops. In 2016 they became illegal and are now only available from dealers or online dealers.

A range of NPS drugs

NPS drugs take the form of pills, powders and smoking mixtures. When you buy packets of an NPS drug you cannot be sure what you are getting. There are four different types of NPS drugs that have different effects.

- Some, like methadone, are stimulants and act like MDMA and amphetamines (see below).

- Others, such as barbiturates, have the opposite effect and act as sedatives or downers.

- Another group, which includes a drug known as 'spice', has a long list of negative side effects.

- The fourth group is hallucinogens (see LSD below), which alter perceptions and cause hallucinations.

Taking NPS drugs is very risky. How dangerous they are depends on what you take, where you take it, how strong it is, whether you mix it with other drugs or alcohol, your own weight and physical condition and how you react to the drug.

Spice

The Drug Enforcement Agency (DEA) in the United States gives the following information on spice:

Spice is a mix of herbs (shredded plant material) and manmade chemicals with mind-altering effects. It is often called 'synthetic marijuana' or 'fake weed' because some of the chemicals in it are similar to ones in marijuana; but its effects are sometimes very different from marijuana, and frequently much stronger. Usually the chemicals are sprayed onto plant materials to make it look like marijuana.

People who have had bad reactions to spice report symptoms like:

- fast heart rate
- throwing up
- feeling anxious or nervous
- feeling confused
- violent behaviour
- suicidal thoughts.

Spice can also raise blood pressure and cause less blood to flow to the heart. In a few cases, it has been linked with heart attacks and death. People who use spice often may have withdrawal and addiction symptoms.

Source: https://teens.drugabuse.gov/drug-facts/spice

Fact check

In the UK, illegal drugs are classified into three main categories: Class A, B or C. The most severe punishments and fines are given for possessing, supplying or producing Class A drugs.

Find out the different classifications of the following drugs and what the penalties are for possessing, supplying and producing each one: cannabis, MDMA, spice, LSD.

LSD

LSD, also known as acid, is a powerful hallucinogenic drug that has unpredictable results. It is swallowed and takes about half an hour to take effect. It distorts reality and the user has a 'trip', which lasts for up to 12 hours. During a trip, a person's feelings and thoughts are altered and their awareness of the world is heightened. If it is a good trip, they will have a pleasant experience, feeling relaxed and happy.

However, acid trips can be very unpleasant. People having a bad trip can become anxious, confused and agitated. There are stories of people who have imagined a world full of spiders and snakes, who have become violent and abusive, and of people who are so convinced that they can fly that they have jumped from windows.

The LSD can leave a person with mental health problems. Users can also have flashbacks during which they relive part of the trip.

If you take LSD, you are taking a gamble – there's no way of knowing whether you'll have a good trip or bad trip.

Ask Erica

Dear Erica

One of my friends says he wants to try taking LSD. What can I say to persuade him not to?

Martyn

Draft Erica's reply to Martyn.

Amphetamines

Amphetamines are Class B drugs which come as an off-white or pinkish coloured powder. They are commonly known as speed and are either swallowed, sniffed or injected.

Amphetamines are stimulants and people who take them feel extra energy and confidence. When the effect wears off they may feel anxious and panicky.

They are addictive both physically and psychologically. People who have become addicted and try to stop taking them can suffer withdrawal symptoms, such as feelings of depression. They are particularly dangerous if taken with alcohol or anti-depressants.

Freddie's story

'I only took speed once, but never again. I was drinking with some friends and thought I'd try it. It made me feel light-headed and full of energy. So I carried on drinking and took some more. But when I got home I felt sick and collapsed on my bed. I lay there wide awake, feeling terrible. Eventually I drifted in and out of sleep. I kept thinking I'd feel better the next day, but I actually felt worse. One of my friends came round and was shocked to see me in such a state. He persuaded me to go to A&E. They told me I could have died from mixing alcohol and speed.'

1. What do you learn about speed from the information about amphetamines and Freddie's story?
2. Why do people take amphetamines?
3. What are the risks involved?

A group of you has been invited to join a panel of experts taking part in a drugs education forum. The people chosen are each to give a short speech about one of the following types of drug: cannabis, MDMA, LSD, amphetamines.

- Decide who is going to give the speeches and, in groups, help them to prepare their speeches by researching the drug they will talk about (effects, risks, statistics).
- Then role play the forum, which should include comments and questions from the audience.

7.3 How can I tell if a drug is safe?

As you have learned on the previous pages, taking drugs can be dangerous.

Legal drugs, such as alcohol, have labels giving details of their contents and strength, so you can tell what you are consuming. However, you don't get that information when you buy illegal drugs like MDMA.

So how can you know if they are safe?

You can't, unless the tablet or powder is tested. This is why some music festivals allow testing centres run by the voluntary organisation 'The Loop' to be set up, so that festival goers planning to take drugs can find out what they contain.

MDMA pills nowadays can be five times as strong as they were in 2009. A standard dose of MDMA is around 80 mg, but some pills now contain as much as 300 mg.

You should also be aware of the risks of taking prescription drugs. You should only ever take prescription drugs if they have been given to you by a doctor who knows your age and medical history, following the instructions on the prescription.

Taking someone else's prescription drugs or buying these kind of drugs online is very dangerous. Some prescription drugs such as opioids (strong painkillers including codeine, methadone and morphine) can be addictive. Others can have serious side effects and be fatal in large doses. Prescription drugs should never be taken with other drugs or alcohol.

Is legalisation the answer?

'I don't think it would help,' says Dr Ramsay, a specialist in drug identification. 'It would make it less likely that people got unexpectedly strong tablets, but it wouldn't stop people taking too many – just like the law doesn't stop people drinking too much.

'What we need is to give people practical casualty avoidance advice, but it's difficult to do that without sounding preachy. The sensible advice is obviously don't take ecstasy – but this is the real world and people are going to.

'If you are going to take it, then the main thing is to be prepared for the possibility that you are going to get a pill which is much stronger than you wanted or anticipated. You don't know how much ecstasy there is in the tablet, so the issue is what you can do about that.

'So be cautious. Take half a tablet, or a quarter of a tablet, and if you're OK after half an hour or so then take a bit more. That way, if you've been given a tablet with 300mg in it, you'll finish up taking a relatively safe dose.

'There's also the advice we've been giving for over 20 years – keep cool, drink plenty of water, try not to overheat. There's definitely an association with heat and MDMA toxicity. It's more toxic if you are hot than if you're not.

'Importantly, look after your mates. If you feel unwell, or if your friend feels unwell, do something about it. Don't ignore it.'

Source: Dr Ramsay's advice adapted from *The Tab* 11/08/2016

What to do in an emergency

Using drugs can be dangerous. It can result in an emergency because you:

- take a drug that is stronger than you thought
- take too much of the drug
- take a drug that's contaminated
- have an unusual reaction to whatever drug you've taken.

If someone feels tense and starts to panic:

- Speak to them calmly and reassure them that the feelings will pass.
- Take them to somewhere quieter and away from any bright lights.
- Tell them that the effects of the drug will gradually wear off.

If they are panicking, they may start to breathe quickly and gasp for breath. This is called hyperventilating. If you can, get a paper bag and place it over their mouth and nose. Get them to breathe into it 6–12 times, then remove the paper bag. After a short pause, repeat as necessary till the hyperventilation stops.

If someone is dehydrated:

- Get them to take a rest from dancing.
- Get them to drink them some water, fruit juice or a sports drink.
- But don't give them too much. About a pint an hour is sufficient. More than that can be dangerous.
- Do not give them alcohol.

If someone is overheating:

- Take them to a cooler area – outside if possible.
- Splash them with cold water to cool them down.
- Take off any warm clothing and any hat they are wearing that will keep heat in.
- Call an ambulance.

If the person becomes drowsy or unconscious:

- Don't lie anyone on a bed who is feeling faint and drowsy. They may lose consciousness.
- Keep talking to them to try to stop them losing consciousness.
- If they become unconscious, put them in the recovery position and call an ambulance.
- If possible, do not leave the person alone. Get someone to stay with them.

Talk about how to give first aid to someone who

a) has a panic attack

b) is dehydrated

c) overheats

d) falls unconscious.

You have been asked to produce a leaflet advising teenagers about how to deal with an emergency if someone is reacting badly to taking drugs. It will be distributed to people as they enter a club. Use the material on this spread to write your leaflet.

7.4 Are you addicted to your mobile phone?

Evidence suggests that some people spend so much time on their mobile phones that they become addicted to them.

Here are some questions that will help you to find out whether you are addicted to your mobile phone.

- Do you spend more time in your room messaging your friends rather than time with your family chatting over a meal or watching TV together?

- Do you spend more time messaging your friends than you do talking to them face to face?

- Do you suffer from 'text neck' – a stiff neck caused by constantly looking down at the screen on your phone?

- Do you feel compelled to look at your phone every five minutes to check for messages because you are afraid of missing out?

- Do you have eye-strain and blurred vision from looking at the screen for too long?

- Do you fiddle with your phone at mealtimes?

- Do you get frantically anxious if you mislay your phone?

If you answered yes to the majority of these questions, then you may be addicted to your mobile phone.

What is smartphone addiction?

Smartphone addiction is when you become so dependent on your mobile phone that you crave the next text or notification like a drug. It has been compared to substance abuse. A leading specialist who treats teenagers who are dependent on their phones says that giving teenagers a smartphone is like giving them a bottle of wine or a gram of cocaine.

The introduction of smartphones is changing the way people relate to one another. There are far fewer face-to-face interactions than there used to be. It's now possible to stay in touch with your friends from wherever you are. You don't need to speak to them as you did when people used the telephone to communicate with one another.

The ability to communicate instantly had brought many advantages. It has speeded up communications and made people's lives easier by making it possible to keep in contact at all times. However, there is a downside. Smartphone addiction can have an effect on both your mental and physical state. You can become so dependent on your phone that you are isolated from the real world.

Your phone can tell you how much time you spend on it each day and each week. You can use this to manage the amount of time you spend online.

Am I addicted to my smartphone?

Dr Emma Russell reveals the warning signs

Dr Emma Russell, Kingston University, says that if you pick up your phone after hearing a ringtone or vibration – even if you are in the middle of something – it could be a sign that you are 'addicted' to your phone.

'We advise reducing notifications by turning off these alerts. If you go straight to your phone after an alert, it's what we call an addictive response,' she said.

The Telegraph, 28 October 2018

Ask Erica

Dear Erica

My friend never pays any real attention to us any more. She's always on her phone – texting people, posting on social media, and posting selfies to Snapchat and Instagram. I am worried that she is becoming addicted to her phone. How can I tell? How can I help her? What should I do?

Felina

Write Erica's reply to Felina.

'The benefits of smartphones outweigh the problems.' Hold a debate on this motion.

When the fun stuff stops being fun

Sharing posts on social media is a fab way of letting people know what your likes and dislikes are, what you think is cool or bang out of order. Sometimes, though, there's a pressure to share posts – some posts specifically say that if you share them something really great will happen, and some say that bad things will happen if you don't pass them on. These are called chain posts. Before chain posts, there were chain e-mails and before there were chain e-mails, there were chain letters. You see, the idea has been around for some time.

Some of them are pretty harmless. If you share this you will have good fortune – but some are really nasty: 'share this post if you love your mum because if you don't she will die.' I know how horrid it can be to get one of these and how much pressure you can feel to share or send on. There is no truth in them, though. No bad thing will happen if you don't send them on and no good thing will happen if you do. They are made up by someone back down the chain who wants to see how far they can go. Ignore, delete or if you're really freaked out about this and feel like you HAVE to pass it on, pass it on to an adult and explain to them why have done this. When you are online it can consume you. I know.

I'm as guilty as anyone of fiddling on my phone, getting hooked on games, obsessively checking social media. I know, too, that it can take me away from what is happening in my real life, around me. One of the things that can get under your skin the most and take over your thoughts is gaming, although the fear of missing something on social media comes a close second. Like all addictions – alcohol, drugs, even exercise – it is bad if it gets to the stage where you can't control it.

From *The Girls' Guide to Growing Up Great* by Sophie Elkan

What do you think of the article above?

- Do you spend too much time on social media?
- Have you ever felt ill or anxious after using a mobile phone?

Talk about your experiences, and what you could do instead, as an alternative to using your mobile phone or to limit the time you spend on it.

8.1 Alcohol: the facts

Alcohol is an intoxicating depressant drug that acts on the central nervous system to slow down the body and brain.

It is a powerful and potentially addictive drug. It usually takes about 5–10 minutes for alcohol to take effect and the effects can last for several hours.

Short-term effects

After one or two drinks, most people feel more relaxed and less inhibited. After several drinks you may start to slur your speech and become clumsy. If you continue to drink, you may be unable to walk straight, you may get double vision, you may become confused or aggressive, or you may vomit and lose consciousness. This can be particularly dangerous as you could choke on your own vomit.

How much the alcohol affects you depends on several factors:

- how quickly you have drunk it and whether you have had anything to eat beforehand (food helps to soak up the alcohol)
- your weight – the smaller you are, the less body fluid you have to dilute the alcohol (this is why girls generally get drunk more quickly than boys)
- what you drink and how much (the alcohol in fizzy drinks like alcopops reaches your brain faster)
- how used to drinking you are (over time the liver learns to break down alcohol faster; this is why it takes very little time to get you drunk at first).

Long-term effects

If you drink heavily over a long period, you can become addicted to alcohol. You run the risk of brain damage, liver disease, mouth and throat cancer, heart problems and stomach ulcers. More than 40 per cent of children who start to drink before they are 13 will go on to abuse alcohol or to become alcoholics at some point in their lives, according to the AlcoHelp website.

Also, since alcohol is made from sugar or starch it is full of calories. One pint of beer contains about 180 calories, almost as much as a large slice of pizza. The calories you get from alcohol have no nutritional value, so drinking alcohol adds nothing to your diet. It also cuts down the amount of fat your body burns for energy.

The strength of alcoholic drinks

The strength of an alcoholic drink is shown on the label by the percentage of pure alcohol it contains (ABV: alcohol by volume). Drinks can be measured in units according to how much alcohol is in them.

How many **units are in common drinks?**

1.6 units	2.3 units	2.6 units	1 unit	1.1 units	2.3 units
1 bottle (330ml) **of premium beer** based on 5% ABV	**1 pint of beer** based on 4% ABV	**1 pint of cider** based on 4.5% ABV	**1 glass of 25ml measured spirits** based on 40% ABV	**1 bottle** (275ml) **of alcopop** based on 4% ABV	**1 medium** (175ml) **glass of wine** based on 18% ABV

drinkaware

Fact check

If you are under 18 it is illegal:

- for you to buy alcohol
- for an adult to buy you alcohol*
- for anyone to sell you alcohol
- for you to drink alcohol in licensed premises (e.g. pubs, restaurants)*.

* If you are 16 or 17 and with an adult you can be bought beer, wine or cider to drink with a meal.

If you are 16 or under you are able to go into many pubs and licenced places with an adult.

Putting alcohol into someone's drink without their knowledge or consent is against the law. Anyone who spikes another person's drink can be charged, fined or sent to prison.

Drinking in public places

If you are under 18, the police can order you to stop drinking in a public place, can confiscate the alcohol and you can be arrested and fined.

If you are over 18 you can drink in public, except in certain areas where there is a Public Space Protection Order (PSPO).

Why do teenagers drink?

A group of teenagers talk about drinking and why they started.

'Everyone in our group drinks. If I didn't they'd think I was a wimp.'

'My parents said drinking is better than taking drugs, so at least I'm not doing something dangerous.'

'All my family drink and it's never done them any harm.'

'I started to drink because of problems at home. When I'm drunk I forget all about them.'

'I'm quite shy. Drinking helps me to lose my inhibitions.'

Talk about what these teenagers say.

1. Did they actually want to start drinking, or were they pressured into it?

2. What might they say to their younger selves now about drinking?

Give reasons for your views.

Different countries have different drinking laws. Out of 190 countries, 61 per cent have a minimum legal drinking age of 18 to 19. The USA has the highest age of 21. In 16 countries, many of which have large Muslim populations, the drinking of alcohol is forbidden.

1. Do you think the age at which you can buy alcohol should be lowered to 16? Give reasons for your views.

2. Should drinking in all public places be forbidden?

Research one of the questions below. Report your findings to the class.

1. What are the laws concerning advertising alcohol to young people? Do they need updating to stop the use of pop-ups in computer games?

2. What is the law about spiking drinks, by adding drugs to them. What are the dangers of this?

8.2 Alcohol: the risks

You have already learned about some of the negative effects of drinking alcohol. There are also other risks that you need to know about.

Alcohol poisoning

According to the AlcoHelp website, every year 1000 under-15s are admitted to hospital needing emergency treatment for acute alcohol poisoning. Some of them die.

Acute intoxication can occur rapidly in young people because of their lower body weight and because it takes longer for the liver to get rid of the alcohol.

If the level of alcohol in your body gets too high it can affect your balance and speech, and it can lower your body temperature, causing hypothermia. It can affect your breathing and heartbeat. You could lose consciousness and choke on your own vomit.

Mixing alcohol with other substances

Alcohol is a drug. Teenagers who drink are more likely to smoke tobacco and cannabis and to use other recreational drugs than those who don't drink. Mixing alcohol with other drugs can be very dangerous. This is particularly the case for alcohol and cocaine.

Accidents

Drinking alcohol affects a person's judgment and coordination, which is why it is against the law to drink and drive. Young people who drink are more likely to get injured and to have an accident than non-drinkers.

Unsafe situations

Drinking alcohol can put young people in dangerous situations where they are vulnerable. They are more likely to have sex without consent or unprotected sex, or to get into a fight and get in trouble with the police. They are also more vulnerable to being mugged or taken advantage of.

Problems at school and with mental health

Alcohol can affect your memory and concentration. Children who start to drink before the age of 13 are more likely to fall behind at school, to miss school and to be excluded.

Young people who drink excessively are more likely to suffer from mental health problems. Many young people who drink say they do so in order to forget their problems.

Sobering up – four dangerous myths

1. Drinking coffee will help you sober up. Untrue. The caffeine in coffee doesn't have any effect on the alcohol you've drunk.

2. You can sleep it off. Untrue. This can be dangerous, because you might lose consciousness.

3. A cold shower will sober you up. Untrue. There is a danger the shock of the cold water makes you lose consciousness.

4. You can walk it off. Untrue. Walking does not increase the rate at which alcohol leaves your body.

Diary of a teenage alcoholic

Amy was 11 when she started drinking.

We were standing outside the off-licence on the estate. We'd seen other kids drinking and thought we'd have a go. It looked like a laugh.

So we asked everyone going inside and eventually someone got us a two-litre bottle of White Lightning – after we gave them our pocket money and paper round cash.

That first taste was horrible, but it didn't stop me. I wanted to feel hard and grown up. And after a few mouthfuls I began to feel a real buzz.

We went back to the offie at least three times on that first day. By the end of the night I was wrecked – I felt really sick and threw up.

But it didn't put me off. We drank most nights from then on – at least three or four nights a week. There was always someone to buy it for us. We'd sit by the bus stop having a smoke and downing cans of beer, cheap cider and sometimes bottles of wine.

Age 12

At school I'd fall asleep, because of the hangovers. Every night we'd be out having a spliff and a few bevies.

I tried to hide it. I'd go home and go straight to bed after brushing my teeth to disguise the smell of the alcohol.

My mum was often in tears. I caused her so much worry, but I didn't care. All I cared about was drinking.

Age 13

I started to feel really down, but I just couldn't see that it was the drinking. There's a lot about those days I can't remember. With all the drinking there are loads of times I've no memory of.

The funny thing is, I never actually liked the taste of alcohol. It was just my way out of things. At first it was fun, then things started happening and it was my escape route. It didn't matter what I was drinking.

My parents were put through so much. I'll always feel guilty.

I became addicted very quickly. And once you're on that path, it's very hard to come back.

The Daily Mirror, 20 February 2007

In groups, imagine you have been commissioned to make a TV programme aimed at young people on the risks of drinking alcohol. Prepare a PowerPoint presentation of your plans for the programme.

Drink wisely

If you do choose to drink alcohol with your friends, follow this advice.

- Eat something before you have any alcohol.

- Take your time. Don't drink quickly in order to keep up with others.

- Don't be pressurised into having a drink you don't want.

- Set yourself a limit of how much you intend to drink in an evening.

- Stick to that limit.

- Don't set out to get drunk.

- Listen to a friend who suggests you've had enough.

- If you start to feel dizzy and light-headed, stop drinking alcohol.

- Have a soft drink or water every other drink.

Discuss the reasons for each piece of advice above. Can you add any others to this list?

On your own, do this quiz, then compare your answers in a class discussion.

1. Wine or beer won't make you as drunk as spirits.

2. Alcohol is a stimulant that increases brain activity.

3. It is dangerous to mix alcohol with ecstasy.

4. Alcoholism is easy to treat.

5. A cup of coffee will help you to sober up.

6. Binge drinking is OK now and then.

7. People who are drunk may do something stupid.

8. Alcohol can cause long-term damage to your liver.

9. Some people get drunk more quickly than others.

10. Teenagers who start drinking before the age of 15 are more likely to become dependent on alcohol as adults.

8.3 Alcoholism

An alcohol addiction is when a person cannot control their drinking. People with alcoholism come from all walks of life and the reasons why people drink vary.

What triggers people to drink heavily may be an event, such as divorce or money troubles, or it may just be a habit that becomes a dependency. Whatever the cause, alcoholism is a disease and the person needs to get treatment.

If someone with an addiction suddenly stops drinking they usually suffer withdrawal symptoms. These include getting 'the shakes' – severe hand tremors – and hallucinating. They also sweat heavily, have difficulty sleeping and get depressed and anxious.

People need support if they are going to give up drinking. Advice and support are available from organisations such as Alcohol Concern and Alcoholics Anonymous.

Signs that a person may have a problem with alcohol

- They have at least two alcoholic drinks every day.
- Once they have had one alcoholic drink they cannot stop themselves having another one.
- They may feel the need for an alcoholic drink to get themselves going in the morning.
- They regularly wake up with a hangover.
- They regularly exceed the number of units recommended for someone of their age, gender and body size.
- They have been out drinking the night before but cannot remember what happened.
- They have fallen over on the way home from a drinking session.
- They refuse to talk about it when someone suggests they have a drink problem.
- They have missed days at school or work because they have felt too ill after a night out.
- They have tried without success to cut down the amount they drink.
- They have had unprotected sex when drunk.
- They have been refused entry to a club because they were drunk.

- They hide alcohol in the house to make sure other people don't find it.
- They lie about how much they drink.
- They become irritable and anxious when they can't have a drink.

Ask Erica

Dear Erica

I'm really worried about a friend. They're drinking all the time now. They never want to do anything else in the evening, and never seem to get up in the morning any more. And they stink of alcohol. I've tried talking to them but they just get defensive about it. What should I do?

Annie

DISCUSS

If this was your friend, what do you think would be the best ways of approaching the problem and helping them?

Living with an alcoholic parent

If a parent has an alcohol addiction, life at home can be very stressful. A teenager with an alcoholic parent may experience a range of emotions.

- **Embarrassment** – They may be embarrassed if their parent is seen drunk in public. They may try to hide the fact that their parent drinks too much from their friends and/or their teacher.
- **Fear** – They may feel apprehensive about how their parent will behave when drunk and what may happen in the future if their parent doesn't stop drinking.
- **Sadness** – They may feel sad that they can no longer relate to the parent in the way they used to.
- **Fault** – They may think that somehow it's their fault that the parent started to drink heavily.
- **Worry** – They may be worried that the parent will turn violent or will have an accident and hurt themselves.
- **Anger** – They may be angry with the parent for causing so much trouble in the family.

How alcoholism affects families

Having an addiction in the family affects how the family functions. The family may get into financial difficulties because the person loses their job and they are unable to pay the bills. They may lose their home because they cannot pay the mortgage or the rent.

The children may be neglected and may suffer emotionally or physically. An older child may have to look after younger brothers and sisters. There are children all over the country acting as carers.

Alcoholism has a profound effect not just on the alcoholic but on all the members of the family.

Tom's story

Tom (16) gets up when his alarm goes off at 6.30 a.m He checks to see if his father has come home and finds him sprawled across the bed half-dressed. Tom showers, gets dressed and gets breakfast for his younger sisters, Dinah (8) and Sara (6). Ever since his mother died 18 months ago and his father's drinking got worse, Tom has taken on the role of carer for his sisters.

He cooks their meals, washes their clothes, gets them off to school, collects them from after-school club, makes sure that Dinah does her homework and that they go to bed on time. He tries to look after his father, too, when he comes home, but lately he hasn't always been doing so. After Dinah and Sara are in bed, Tom clears up the kitchen and then does his own homework.

Weekends he spends doing the shopping and other chores, then catching up with his own homework. He rarely goes out with his friends. He doesn't want his sisters to be taken into care, but he's constantly worried that they will be. He wishes he could turn the clock back to before his father drank so much.

Valerie's story

'My earliest memories are of my mother shouting at my father. They rowed every night because my mother was an alcoholic. I remember my father pulling me into the bedroom and locking the door and my mother banging on the door in a drunken rage. I was terrified of her. She would look at me with hatred and say she wished I'd never been born.

'I would lie awake at night listening to them shouting and screaming. Or I'd climb into the wardrobe and shut the door. Then I'd curl up with my hands over my ears to try to block out her screams. I once asked my grandmother if I could go and live with her, but she said my mother wouldn't allow it. The abuse only ended when she knocked my father down the stairs and they took me into care.'

In groups, discuss how Tom's and Valerie's lives have been affected by alcoholism.

Find out what support is available for young people like Tom and Valerie, and their parents. You could visit websites for the National Association for Children of Alcoholic Parents, Drinkaware, ADAM (Another's Drinking Affects Me), Alcoholics Anonymous and Al-Anon Family Groups.

9.1 Immunisations and health checks

As a young adult you will want to start to take responsibility for your own health. It is important to protect yourself against infectious diseases.

There are many ways you can catch infectious diseases:

- by breathing in droplets that are coughed, sneezed or breathed out by an infected person
- by direct contact, touching an infected person or touching a surface an infected person has touched
- by eating contaminated food or drinking polluted water
- from insects, such as flies and mosquitoes, and animals that spread diseases, such as rats.

Washing your hands with soap and hot water, sneezing and coughing into a tissue, and regularly disinfecting surfaces can all help to stop the spread of infectious diseases.

Infectious diseases are caused by three types of microbe – bacteria, viruses and fungi. Bacterial infections can be treated with antibiotics; viruses cannot. This is why your doctor will not prescribe antibiotics for viruses like colds, flu, chickenpox or measles.

Immunisation

In the past, children often caught infectious diseases, such as mumps and measles. Today, very young children are given vaccines to prevent this. Vaccines work by inserting a weakened or dead form of the disease into the body. This makes the body's immune system produce antibodies, which destroy the microbes that cause infectious diseases. Memory cells are formed inside the body which will produce the same antibodies if the live form of the microbe ever enters the body. Vaccines are used against diseases which cannot be treated effectively.

The use of such vaccines is called immunisation. The immunisation programme provided by the NHS has proved very effective. The vaccines children are given by the NHS in 2019 include the following.

- The 6-in-one vaccine protects against diphtheria, tetanus, whooping cough, polio, Hib (Haemophilus influenzae type b) and hepatitis B. It is given at 8, 12 and 16 weeks of age to all babies.
- The pneumococcal or pneumo jab (PCV) protects against some types of pneumococcal infection. It is given at 12 weeks and 1 year of age.
- The Rotavirus vaccine protects against rotavirus infection, a common cause of childhood diarrhoea and sickness. It is given at 8 and 12 weeks of age.
- The Men B vaccine protects against meningitis (caused by meningococcal type B bacteria) and is given at 8 weeks, 16 weeks and 1 year of age.
- The Hib/Men C vaccine protects against Haemophilus influenzae type b (Hib) and meningitis caused by meningococcal group C bacteria. It is given at 1 year of age.
- The MMR vaccine protects against measles, mumps and rubella. It is given at 1 year and at 3 years and 4 months of age. (If you catch rubella when you are pregnant, it can seriously damage your unborn baby, causing problems with its sight, brain, hearing or heart.)
- The children's flu vaccine protects against flu. It is given annually as a nasal spray in September or October to all children aged 2 to 11 years.

- Young people aged 12 to 13 are also offered the HPV vaccine, which offers protection against the virus which causes cervical cancer as well as mouth, throat, genital and anal cancers. It also gives protection against genital warts.

1. Why is it important for babies to be immunised against diseases such as polio?

2. What is the HPV vaccination? Why is it offered to all teenagers in Year 8 or Year 9?

3. What would you say to someone who doesn't want to be vaccinated? Why?

Routine checks

Breast cancer

Although about 12.5 per cent of women will develop breast cancer during their lives, it is very rare among teenagers. However, since breast development often begins as a lump under the nipple, teenage girls can worry that something is wrong, especially as these breast buds may be sensitive. To check your breasts, first look in the mirror to see if there are any visible lumps, puckering of the skin or if the nipple has been pulled in slightly. Then lie down, and use the underside of your fingers to press down on your breasts to feel for any lumps. If you can feel anything, check on the other breast to see if there is also a lump there. If you are concerned in any way about changes to your breasts, see a doctor.

Testicular cancer

Testicular cancer is the most common form of cancer among males aged 15–34, so it is a good idea to examine yourself regularly – once a month. A good time to carry out an examination is after a bath or shower. The skin around the testicles will be loose. Hold the testicle between the thumb, index and middle finger and roll it gently to search for any lumps. If your testicle feels different, seek medical advice.

The good news is that testicular cancer is entirely curable, but the sooner it is caught the better. Often the cure is to remove the testicle. Doing so does not affect a person's ability to enjoy a normal sex life or to have children.

Thrush

Thrush is very common and affects about 75 per cent of women at some point in their lives. It is caused by an increase in the yeast-like fungi called candida that are found in the vagina.

Symptoms of thrush are:

- a thick white or creamy vaginal discharge
- itching redness, swelling and irritation around the vagina and vulva
- a burning feeling when urinating.

Thrush can develop as a result of taking antibiotics.

It can be cured easily by a course of tablets, by using an anti-fungal cream or a pessary – a pill that is inserted in the vagina.

There are several things you can do to reduce your chances of getting thrush.

- Avoid synthetic underwear and tights. They create a heat trap for the fungi to flourish in.
- Wear clean cotton underwear each day.
- Don't use scented soaps, bubble-bath, bath salts or vaginal deodorants.

Men can also get thrush. Symptoms include:

- redness and swelling on tip of the penis
- a white discharge
- difficulty in pulling back the foreskin.

Again, it can be treated with a cream or course of tablets from a pharmacist.

Ask Erica

Dear Erica

I think I've got thrush. How can I tell? Can I treat it myself?

Shannon

Draft Erica's reply to Shannon.

9.2 Allergies

An allergy is an over-reaction of the body's immune system when it comes into contact with a substance that is usually harmless to other people.

Most allergies are mild, causing symptoms such as a runny nose, watery eyes, sneezing and itching, which can be treated by drugs either on prescription or bought at a pharmacy.

What causes an allergic reaction?

A substance that triggers an allergic reaction is called an allergen.

- Some people react to airborne allergens such as pollen or dust.

- Others have a reaction to the substances in certain foods, such as nuts, shellfish, milk or strawberries.

- About one in ten people suffer an allergic reaction to the sting of a wasp or bee.

- Some people are allergic to certain drugs, such as penicillin.

- People can also be allergic to things they touch, such as certain clothing materials, animal's fur, particular plants or cleaning products.

- Traffic fumes can also trigger an allergy.

Anaphylactic shock

Anaphylactic shock is a severe allergic reaction which can be triggered by an insect sting, certain drugs, such as penicillin, or certain foods, such as nuts. It can be fatal and requires urgent treatment as the person's blood pressure drops and they have difficulty breathing. They require oxygen and a life-saving injection of adrenaline.

A person who is liable to suffer from anaphylactic shock can be given an auto-injector to carry so that they can be injected if they get stung or eat some food to which they are allergic. The auto-injector contains adrenaline.

In 2016, Natasha Ednan-Laperouse died after eating a baguette she bought at Pret a Manger.

The baguette contained sesame seeds, to which she was allergic and which caused her to go into anaphylactic shock. There was no warning label on the baguette and Natasha thought it was safe for her to eat it. Although her father injected her with an epi-pen he could not save her.

Her family successfully campaigned for the law to be changed so that all pre-packed food must be clearly labelled if it contains an allergen.

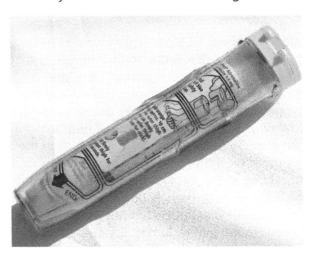

Research what action is being taken to ensure that this new law (introduced in 2019) is being enforced.

Skin allergies — eczema

- Eczema is an allergic reaction in which the skin becomes inflamed. Most eczema causes a red rash and intense itching. Sometimes it can cause blisters.

- It can be caused by an allergic reaction to a food, such as milk, or it may be triggered by something that has been touched or breathed in.

- Eczema can be treated with creams from your pharmacist to get rid of the rash. If scratched, the skin can become infected and a course of antibiotics may be needed.

- It is not contagious so you cannot catch eczema from touching a person who has it.
- Seventy per cent of people who have allergic eczema have a close relative who has it.

Respiratory allergies – hay fever

Hay fever is an allergic reaction to pollen which occurs when the pollen count is high. (Similar reactions can also be caused by house dust mites, animal fur and mould spores.)

Symptoms of hay fever include frequent sneezing, an itchy, blocked or runny nose and red, itchy, watery eyes. Some people also get headaches.

Hay fever (and other allergic rhinitis symptoms) can be treated with medicines that you can obtain from a pharmacist. These consist of antihistamines taken as tablets, syrup, eye drops or sprays. The medicines reduce the effect of the chemical called histamine which your body produces in reaction to the pollen (or other allergen).

Asthma

Asthma is a condition which causes difficulty in breathing because the small tubes (bronchioles) in the lungs have swollen and the airways narrowed. Asthma attacks are often triggered by an allergic reaction.

Many people with asthma control it by using inhalers. There are two types of inhaler – one that gives drugs to prevent asthma occurring and one to provide relief during an attack.

How to help someone who has an asthma attack.

1. Make them comfortable. Get them to sit or stand leaning slightly forwards and tell them to take slow, deep breaths.
2. Help them to find and use their reliever inhaler, which is usually blue.
3. Reassure them that the inhaler should take effect within minutes.
4. If after 5–10 minutes their condition has not improved, seek medical help.

Managing allergies

Identify exactly what your symptoms are, then ask yourself:

- When do the symptoms occur?
- Are they triggered by something you have had to eat or drink?
- Have you just started to use a new product, such as a new soap, shampoo or deodorant?
- Do the symptoms occur when you are in a particular place – in the garden when the grass has just been cut or when you are near particular plants?
- Do they occur when you are near someone who is smoking?

Once you have identified when and where you come into contact with the allergen that causes your symptoms you can take steps to avoid it. You can stay indoors with the windows closed when the pollen count is high. You can avoid stroking the cat if you are allergic to its fur.

One thing you can do is to keep a diary of any symptoms, to look for possible triggers, and to see a doctor if the symptoms persist or if you have any concerns.

1. What causes hay fever? What are its symptoms? How can it be treated?
2. What is asthma? How do people with asthma try to control it? What should you do to help someone who has an asthma attack?
3. What causes eczema? How can it be treated?

1. How much do you know about people in the school who have allergies? What is the school's policy on informing you about any of your peers who have a serious allergy?
2. Produce a leaflet offering advice and information about what to do if someone has a severe allergic reaction.

10.1 Looking after your skin

Your skin has several important functions. It helps to protect your body from infections and to control your body's temperature, so it's important to look after it.

Keeping your skin clean

Germs can get on your skin, particularly on your hands. You can keep them clean by washing them. Use warm water and a mild soap.

You should wash your face, under your arms and your genitals daily. You will see shelves full of skin care products in pharmacies but as a young person you should only need a cleanser, rather than anything harsh or anti-ageing.

Acne: the facts

Acne is a skin condition that produces a variety of spots, usually on the face, but also sometimes on the back and the top of the chest.

It occurs during adolescence when an excess of oil is produced by the glands under the skin as a reaction to the changing levels of hormones. This causes the pores in the skin and hair follicles to get blocked. This leads to an infection at the bottom of the blockage and produces spots.

Acne is not caused by poor personal hygiene, eating too much chocolate or greasy foods. It cannot be cured by sunbathing, but it can be treated. There is no single treatment that works for everybody.

How to deal with acne

- Wash your face and other affected areas twice a day with lukewarm water and a mild soap. Don't wash it more than that as you may irritate the skin and make it worse.

- Do not squeeze spots. This can make them worse and can result in permanent scarring.

- Avoid using make-up to hide them. Choose water-based make up rather than oil-based products.

- Ask your pharmacist for advice on which creams to use.

- If your acne is severe, you may need to see your doctor and have a course of treatment. Treatments may take up to three months to work. Generally, they will produce good results.

Rose's story

'I was 12 when I first started getting acne. I had worse spots than anyone else my age and as I got older, while other people's cleared up, mine got worse.

'I got really badly bullied at school because of my skin. I was constantly teased by this group of girls who told everyone I had chicken pox even though they knew I didn't. They called me ugly and all sorts of nasty names. It was devastating.'

DISCUSS

What do you learn from Rose's story about what it feels like to have severe acne?

ROLE PLAY

Act out a scene in pairs in which one of you challenges the other who has been bullying a person with acne. Ask: 'How would you like it?'

YOUR CHOICE

Some of these statements are facts. Some are myths. On your own, decide which you think are true and which you think are false. Then compare your answers with other people's.

1. Acne is very common in teenagers. About 80 per cent of teenagers get some degree of acne.

2. Acne is contagious. You catch it from coming into contact with someone who has it.

3. You should wash your face regularly and often if you have acne.

4. More boys than girls have acne.

5. The best way to get rid of acne is to squeeze your spots.

6. People with bad acne often get bullied.

7. You shouldn't wear make-up if you have acne.

8. Sweating does not cause acne but it can make it worse.

Tanning

Sunlight is good for you. It provides you with vitamin D which your body needs to stay healthy. However, too much exposure to the Sun's rays can damage your skin and cause skin cancer.

Fact check

- Skin cancer is the most common cancer in the UK.

- Over 100 000 people are diagnosed with skin cancer each year.

- Most skin cancers are curable. Treatment usually involves surgery which can be disfiguring.

- The most dangerous type of skin cancer is malignant melanoma, which is responsible for 2500 deaths a year.

- Skin cancer is usually caused by ultraviolet radiation, either from the sun or from a sunbed. Over-exposure to UV rays can cause sunburn and wrinkles.

UV photograph showing sun-damage which is much less visible to the naked eye.

ROLE PLAY

In pairs, act out a scene in which a teenager argues with a parent or carer who is trying to persuade them to put on sun cream before sunbathing.

DISCUSS

'People say that a suntan makes you look attractive and feel healthy. But when you consider that it fades and can cause damage to your skin, is it worth it?'

In groups, say why you agree or disagree with this view.

Stay safe in the sun

Follow these simple tips to stay safe in the sun.

- Wear clothes that cover up parts of your body that otherwise might get sunburned.

- Wear a hat with a wide brim. Take special care of your ears and neck as these are the most common places for cancers.

- Use a sunscreen that has an SPF (sun protection factor) of at least 30. If it is very hot, or you are fair skinned, you need to use one with a higher SPF. Put it on at regular intervals.

- Use a sunscreen with a UVA rating of 4 or 5 stars. This will give you protection against the harmful ultraviolet rays which can damage your skin and can lead eventually to cancer.

- Avoid being out when the sun is at its hottest from 10 a.m. to 4 p.m.

- Limit the time you spend out in the sun.

- Remember that you need to protect yourself even on a cloudy day, as the sun's rays can penetrate through clouds.

10.2 Caring for your teeth, ears and eyes

Our teeth, ears and eyes are crucial to our quality of life, and if we are lucky enough to have heathy teeth, ears and eyes we should do our best to take care of them.

Tooth decay and gum disease

It is important to look after your teeth to prevent tooth decay, which is caused by plaque, a film of bacteria and saliva that forms on your teeth. Some bacteria in the plaque mix with sugars in the food you eat to form acids. These attack the tooth enamel and cause tooth decay. If it's not treated, the nerve of the tooth can become infected and an abscess may develop. You may have to have the tooth removed.

Plaque can also form on your gums and cause them to bleed. In teenagers this can lead to gingivitis, an inflammation of the gums, which is an early sign of gum disease found in many adults.

In people with advanced gum disease, the plaque forms a hard substance called calculus (also known as tartar). This can irritate the gums so much that they begin to separate from the teeth. The gaps can then fill with bacteria, which attack the gums and loosen the teeth.

Bad breath, sinus trouble and headaches can all be caused by bad teeth.

Top tips for healthy teeth

- See a dentist for regular check-ups. Dental treatment is free for anyone under the age of 18.

- Brush your teeth before you go to bed and at least one other time a day and make sure you change your toothbrush regularly. A worn-out toothbrush with bent bristles won't clean your teeth properly.

- Reduce the risk of gum disease by using dental floss. This will remove bits of food that are trapped between your teeth which your toothbrush can't reach.

- Cut down on sugary snacks and drinks to lessen the amount of plaque that builds up on your teeth.

- Use a toothpaste with fluoride.

ROLE PLAY

'My gums are swollen and bleed when I brush them. But I don't like going to the dentist,' says Alan.

Act out a scene in which a friend tries to find out why Alan doesn't like going to the dentist and then to persuade him to go.

WRITE

Prepare a dental care factsheet to distribute to children aged 8–11 at a local junior school.

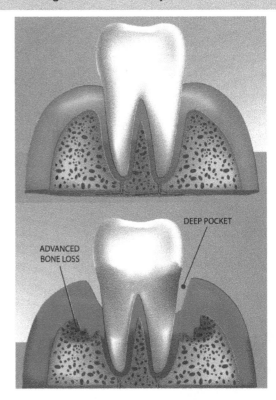

DEEP POCKET

ADVANCED BONE LOSS

Caring for your ears

Listening to loud music can cause permanent damage to your ears, resulting in hearing loss and tinnitus, says Natalie Johnson.

Prolonged exposure to very loud music can permanently damage your ears. The charity Action on Hearing Loss estimates that four million people are at risk of hearing damage from over-amplified music.

Noise levels are measured in decibels. Any noise above 85 decibels can harm the hair cells in your ears and cause hearing loss. The noise level at a concert or festival can be 120 decibels and at clubs is between 110 and 120 decibels.

About one in ten adults suffer from tinnitus – a ringing or buzzing sound in one or both ears even though there is no external source. Many people who attend rock concerts will experience it for a period of several hours after the event.

Up to 90% of the people who suffer from tinnitus have hearing loss resulting from having been exposed to loud noise.

What can you do to protect your ears?

When the sound level is over 100 decibels, as it is in many clubs, it is only safe to listen to the music for 15 minutes. So if you are going to a club, a gig or a concert, wear earplugs. You can buy earplugs that reduce the level of the sound entering your ear but filter the music and do not affect the listening experience. Earplugs are the only things that can protect your ears. Putting cotton wool in your ears does not reduce the level of sound to a safe level.

Make sure, too, that you stand well away from the loudspeakers.

When you are listening to music on your own, use noise cancelling earphones and do not listen for very long periods without taking a break. You should take a break of at least 5 minutes every hour.

Source: Action on Hearing Loss

1. How can loud music damage your ears?
2. What can you do to protect your ears when you go to a concert?

Caring for your eyes

It is important to have your eyes tested regularly. Eye tests can detect problems you may not be aware of, because your eyes are not hurting.

It is important to protect your eyes from bright sunlight by wearing sunglasses that offer protection from UV rays that can damage your eyes.

First aid for eyes

- If you get something in your eye, don't rub it. Gently grip your upper eyelid and pull it over your lower eyelashes. This will produce tears which will wash the object out.
- If something such as a splinter of wood or glass is embedded in an eye, do not try to pull it out. You may cause irreversible damage to the eye by trying to remove it.
- If a chemical or liquid has got into an eye, splash cool water on it for at least 15 minutes to try to wash it out. Don't wipe it with a cloth, as the material may damage the eye.
- If an eye is cut or scratched, don't bathe it or put anything on it.

Once you have applied first aid, get the person to a hospital to have their eyes checked.

1. Design a poster on why you should wear sunglasses, listing the top three ways they can help you.
2. A friend has asked you what sunglasses to buy that will be fashionable but will offer protection for their eyes. Research which ones you would recommend and how much they will cost.

10.3 Caring for your feet and your back

Many adults suffer from problems with their feet and backs for a variety of reasons. It is important as teenagers to look after your feet and back in order to avoid potential problems in the future.

Fact check

Each foot consists of 26 small, delicate bones with many ligaments and muscles. Your feet are specially designed to support the weight of your body. They are subject to greater pressure and more injury than any other part of the body.

Common foot problems

- **Corns** are small areas of hardened skin on the tops of toes, which press inward and can be very painful. They are caused by friction and pressure, usually from badly fitting shoes. You can buy corn plasters from your pharmacist to reduce the pressure on the sore part.

- **Calluses** are areas of hardened skin, which can make walking painful. They are also caused by pressure from shoes.

- **Verrucas** are warts that occur on the sole of the foot. They are contagious and are caused by a virus, which is often picked up in swimming pools. They tend to spread if they are untreated, so ask your pharmacist for a cream to put on them and see your doctor if they persist.

- **Bunions** are painful swellings of the big toe joint. They are a hereditary problem, made worse by badly fitting shoes.

- **Athlete's foot** is a skin disease which results in patches of white, flaking skin and causes itching and burning. It is caused by a fungus, which thrives on warm, moist skin. It can be treated with anti-fungal powder or cream.

- **In-growing toenails** are usually caused by incorrect trimming. When the nail grows, it grows into the flesh of the toe, causing painful swelling.

Top tips for healthy feet

- Always wear comfortable well-fitting shoes.
- Avoid wearing high-heels and platform shoes.
- Keep your feet clean.
- Always cut your toenails straight across.
- Do not cut corns, calluses or ingrowing toenails yourself.
- Consult a pharmacist or doctor before using anything for a foot problem.

DISCUSS

'Children should be allowed to wear whatever shoes they like to school.'

Discuss this view, saying why you agree or disagree.

RESEARCH

1. What are the most common foot injuries?
2. How are they treated?
3. How could the foot injuries be prevented?

Ask Erica

Dear Erica

My parents won't let me wear high heels or platform shoes. They make me wear 'sensible' shoes. My friends' parents let them wear whatever they like. The shoes I have are so unfashionable. How can I persuade my parents that they are being unfair?

Kelly

Write Erica's reply to Kelly.

Looking after your back

Back pain may result from poor posture, weak abdominal or back muscles, or sudden muscle strain, often caused by lifting or carrying heavy objects. Looking after your back in adolescence is important because studies suggest that teenagers who suffer back pain are more likely to develop back pain in later life.

Fact check

A survey carried out by Back Care found that some students were carrying up to 30 per cent of their bodyweight to school each day in the form of books and equipment. Back Care's recommended maximum is 10 per cent of bodyweight.

Lighten the load

- Only take to school the books and equipment you need for that particular day. Leave the rest at home or in your school locker.

- Pack your rucksack carefully. Put heavier items like textbooks on the inside where they will be next to your back; put lighter, smaller items like pens and calculators towards the outside.

- Choose a rucksack with two wide shoulder straps and always wear both straps over your shoulders.

- Make sure that you tighten both straps, so the weight is distributed evenly and the rucksack is not pulling against you as you walk.

- Take off the rucksack carefully, so that you don't put a strain on one side of your body.

How to lift heavy objects

The most common cause of back injuries is lifting heavy objects and putting too much strain on the back. If you lift something awkwardly or too quickly you may damage your spine.

1. Before you lift a heavy object, remove any obstacles that may be in the way.

2. Always keep a straight back when lifting, pulling or pushing. Bend your knees, not your back.

3. Keep what you are lifting as close to your body as possible.

4. Grip the object firmly and straighten your legs to lift the object.

5. Never attempt to lift an object which is too heavy for you.

Sit properly

When you are sitting at a desk or worktop doing your homework or using a computer, your feet should be on the ground or a footrest and your hips level with your knees. The desk should be at elbow height and your eyes level with the top of the computer screen. The chair should have a back, so that your back is supported.

Do not spend too much time sitting in one position. Take regular breaks and stretch your back.

- Do you spend a long time sitting in front of a computer? Does your chair support your back? Is it at the right height?

- Do you carry your schoolbag in a way that could damage your back? Could you make it lighter?

- Are you always careful to lift heavy objects properly?

Discuss how you might change what you do in order to avoid back problems in the future.

10.4 Tattoos and piercings

For thousands of years, people in different parts of the world have had their bodies tattooed and pierced. Recently, tattoos and piercings have become more fashionable in our society. It is important to take care when getting a tattoo or piercing.

Tattoos

More and more young people are choosing to have tattoos. There are lots of different reasons for this.

- Young people get tattoos because they think it makes them look cool and sexy.
- Some people get a tattoo to cover up a scar or blemish on their skin.
- Teenagers may get a tattoo as a sign of their individuality, to make themselves look different.

- Some teenagers get tattoos as a way of rebelling.
- Some people get tattooed because they like the design and want to have it on their body.
- A couple may get tattoos as a way of showing their commitment to each other, or parents to show their love for their children, like David Beckham.
- Some people get a tattoo to show that they belong to a particular group.

If you are thinking of getting a tattoo

Make sure you go to a licensed tattoo parlour, where the equipment is sterilised, where the tattooist washes their hands and wears gloves and the needles are clean. You could get HIV or hepatitis from dirty needles. (*For more information about HIV see Unit 4.2.*)

Before you get a tattoo, ask yourself:

- Why do I want a tattoo?
- Am I doing this for myself or because someone else wants me to do it?
- Is anyone putting pressure on me to have a tattoo?
- Will I regret having a tattoo?
- How will I feel about it in a year, five years' or ten years' time?
- What if I want to have it removed? Will I be able to afford it? Will it hurt?
- What if my skin stretches because I put on weight, grow taller or have a baby?

Fact check

It is against the law to tattoo anyone under 18, but many tattoo parlours do not ask for proof of age.

Discuss

1. Study the list of reasons why people get tattoos. What do you think is the most common reason? Can you suggest any other reasons?
2. Should tattoo parlours be made to ask for proof of age, or should you be able to get a tattoo at any age?

Body piercing

As mentioned earlier, body piercing has been part of many cultures for thousands of years. In some cultures, it is regarded as a rite of passage in which a teenager becomes an adult or it is performed on an individual in recognition of their great courage.

Eyebrow piercing was introduced more recently as a fashion statement by the punk rock movement of the 1970s.

An increasing number of people in today's societies are choosing to have parts of their body pierced.

Fact check

Until recently there were no laws about having piercings, so people who chose to do so could have their noses, tongues, eyebrows, navel, nipples or genitals pierced. In 2018, however, a law came into force in Wales making it illegal to pierce the tongue, nipples or genitals of anyone under 18.

1. What is the significance of tattoos and piercings in New Zealand, which has the highest number of tattoos per person in the world?

2. Use the internet to research the Maori peoples, and why tattoos and/or piercings are culturally important to that group.

1. Should the new law about piercing the tongue, nipples or genitals be introduced in the rest of the UK?

2. Should there be laws about the ages at which the nose, navel and eyebrows can be pierced?

Tongue piercing

Before you get your tongue or lip pierced, you need to consider the risks, such as the risk of infection.

In addition, it can be harmful for your teeth and gums, causing cracked or chipped teeth through contact with the jewellery. The jewellery may also rub against the enamel and damage your teeth. It can rub against your gums and cause gum disease, leading to gum recession which is very serious and can lead to tooth loss.

It's little wonder that dentists advise you not to meddle with your mouth.

Act out a conversation in which a dentist explains to a patient why they would advise them against getting their tongue pierced.

Ask Erica

Dear Erica

I'm thinking of getting a piercing where it won't show. What things do I need to consider before I get my nipples or my navel pierced?

Maria

1. Draft Erica's reply to Maria.

2. Write an article giving teenagers advice on what they need to think about before getting a tattoo or piercing.

11.1 Dealing with anger

Anger is defined as a strong feeling of annoyance, displeasure or hostility.

Often people who are angry describe a loss of control. This can lead you to behaving in an emotional rather than a rational way.

There are several different ways of dealing with anger. These include identifying what makes you angry, thinking about what to do when you feel angry, and dealing with anger after the event.

What makes you angry?

'I get angry when I feel I'm being treated unfairly. This usually happens with my parents, who compare me with my brother. My brother is older than me, so he gets to do different things from me. Yet my parents expect me to behave the same as him.'
Jaz, Portsmouth

'I'm a perfectionist. I get angry when things don't work out. If I'm working on a school project and something goes wrong, I'll just flip.'
Callum, Norwich

'I get angry when friends let me down. If a friend stands me up and doesn't apologise it will make me cross.'
Anna, Sunderland

'I get really angry when someone stares at me and disrespects me.'
Angela, Swansea

WRITE

Write one or two sentences saying what makes you angry.

DISCUSS

1. In groups, look at the statements above. Discuss what makes each of the people angry.

2. Share what you have written about what makes you angry. Talk about whether there are any things you need to avoid, such as particular:

   • situations   • places   • people.

Anger reservoir

'I get angry about little things. The bus might be late so it gets to me a bit. Then it's raining, so it will get to me a bit more. Then somebody will shake their umbrella and get me wet. The trouble is that I store anger in my body. Eventually, it will all come out.'
Nadia, Glasgow

Read Nadia's statement above. Her body is like a container which gradually fills up with anger. She has a big anger reservoir as it takes quite a lot to wind her up before she loses her temper. However, she has nowhere for her anger to go, so it builds up until she loses her temper. For Nadia, anger is like stress – she holds it in her body. It needs some sort of release.

'I get angry when I'm tired and have had a long day. Then I've got a short fuse and can kick off at anything.'
Lisa, Belfast

Everyone is different. Some people with a small anger reservoir can get angry very quickly. This can be over the smallest things.

People get angry in all sorts of situations. Sometimes it's because of an argument. Sometimes it can be because they forget something, or because somebody else does something. The important thing is to recognise when your anger reservoir is almost full, and those things that make you angry easily, so you can do something about it.

Anger can be a sign that you are not happy with a situation or with someone's behaviour. The challenge is what to do with our anger when we feel it.

What to do when you get angry

Sometimes we find ourselves angry when we are in an argument. There is a saying in that, 'It takes two people to argue – one to start it and one to finish it.'

If you have lost your temper, you are likely to say things that you don't mean and not respond rationally to what is going on. The best thing to do is to stop the argument, let both of you calm down, and then continue the discussion later. There are several ways of doing this.

- Go to the toilet. This creates a break in proceedings.

- Walk away, ignoring negative comments from the other person.

- Tell the other person that you need some time out now, but will talk to them again later.

ROLE PLAY

Imagine you are having an argument with a friend about what you want to do this weekend. In threes, role play the argument. Two of you should argue, while the third person observes. Then swap round, so everyone has a turn arguing and observing. Then discuss what you noticed when you were observing, and what helped you deal with the issues in the argument.

After an argument

After an argument, it is important to recognise how you feel. If the argument was with a friend, sibling, parent or carer it is important to make up. You should:

- Apologise, regardless of whether or not the other person was wrong. Say, 'I'm sorry' rather than, 'I'm sorry but …' Adding a 'but' risks continuing the argument.

- Listen carefully to what the other person is saying. There is always more than one perspective in a situation. You may have missed something important they said.

- Analyse what really happened. This is because there are actually three perspectives in any situation – your perspective, that of the person

you were arguing with, and what really happened. It can be useful to discuss what happened with an independent third person.

- Treat the situation as a learning experience. We can't change other people's behaviour, but we can change our own. There is always room to learn. What would you do differently next time?

- Even if you have not resolved the situation, put it behind you. Anger only exists in the present. It is better for you and your health to just let it go.

- If something is still bothering you after an argument, apply the five-year rule to it: think, will it still be bothering you in five years' time? If not, it is time to let it go.

DISCUSS

In groups, discuss which you think is the best advice for after an argument. Give reasons for your views.

Anger

Anger
Is a red bull
Charging through the mind's fields
Inciting actions you may soon
Regret

By John Foster

DISCUSS

Read the poem above. What does it tell you about anger? Give reasons for your views.

WRITE

Write a cinquaine (a five-line poem like the one above) describing how you feel when you're angry. (To follow the form, use two syllables in line one, four syllables in line two, six syllables in line three, eight syllables in line four and two syllables in line five.)

11.2 Jealousy

Jealousy is a negative emotion that we can feel in a variety of situations.

Jealousy can include feelings of insecurity, concern and envy. It can also include a fear of missing out because you don't have something. Often, jealousy is felt when you compare yourself to someone else.

Dealing with jealousy

Jealousy can be like a disease, in that it can infect the way you think and feel. However, jealousy can also be treated like a disease, by 'vaccinating' yourself against it. Thinking about what makes you jealous in the first place is a good start.

'I live on an estate and we don't have a lot of money. I'm always jealous of the rich kids who have more money than me and can do what they like in life.'
Joe, Bournemouth

'My best friend always seems to have a boyfriend, and I don't. I get really annoyed when I see them together because I'm so jealous.'
Chloe, Ipswich

'I wish I was better at sports. There's this one guy on the team who is a much better footballer than me. I wish I could be like him.'
John, Aberdeen

'There's this girl at school who always seems to be surrounded by friends and is really popular. I've only got one or two friends at school. I wish I was popular too.'
Tamsin, Lancaster

'I'm jealous of my older brother, because he always gets to try new things before me.'
Connie, Craigavon

'I hate it that there's always some kid at school wearing the latest expensive trainers and I can't afford them.'
Tariq, Leicester

DISCUSS

In groups, look at the situations opposite.

1. What makes each of the people jealous and why?

2. What makes you feel jealous?

Protecting yourself against jealousy

There are several different ways to protect yourself against jealousy. Here are some them.

- Put things into perspective. There are billions of people in the world and there will always be somebody who is better than you at something or in some way. The important thing is to realise this and to acknowledge that it's not the most important thing. You may have skills or attributes that other people don't have.

- Recognise that the situation is only temporary. You won't always be at school – you may go on to college, university, an apprenticeship or a job. You won't always have the same number of friends – this will change over time, as your situation changes. The amount of money you have in life can change – depending on how hard you work towards your exams or what sort of job you get. Change the jealousy around by recognising what you want in life – whether it's more money, more free time, or to make more friends. Make this a positive goal.

- Recognise that if something is unfair, there are things you can do to address it. If you have brothers or sisters, and you feel your parents are treating you differently, talk to them about it. Often, your parents will have very good reasons for doing so. Older children may be allowed try things out first – like going to the cinema on their own, or going to a party – because they are older. So talk things through so you can see things from everyone's perspective.

When you're feeling jealous

When you're feeling jealous, recognise that you may not be thinking rationally with your head, because your heart wants something really strongly. Take a break from the situation by thinking about something else or doing something that makes you happy. Talk to a third person – whether it's a friend, a teacher or a parent/carer – about the situation, and ask their advice on how they would cope. Try to recognise what you have and work on being grateful for those things.

Dealing with jealous friends

If you suspect a friend is feeling jealous, it's good to find out whether you're right. They may be feeling jealous of you, of somebody else or of a situation.

If they are jealous of a situation or somebody else, then this is easier for you to deal with. Ask your friend if they are OK, and if they would like to talk about the situation. If they are able to open up, talk to them about what makes them jealous, help them put it in perspective and to find a way of dealing with their jealousy.

However, if it is you they are jealous of, you need to be more careful. You may wish to speak to a third person, such as a parent, carer, teacher or another friend before you talk to the friend who is jealous. Don't confront them directly about it. Instead, ask them indirectly what is wrong and if there is anything they would like to talk about.

If you know what they are jealous of, take steps to minimise the jealousy. If they are jealous of your money or what you wear, avoid flaunting your money or new clothes in their face. If they are jealous of your new partner or free time, avoid talking to them about this a lot.

Remember, though, that someone else's jealousy is not caused by you. You can be sensitive to other people's feelings, but they should own their feelings and ultimately be responsible for dealing with them, as you should be with yours.

11.3 Dealing with fear

Fear is a natural emotion that can be caused by believing that something is going to harm us in some way. Often, this can be irrational – you feel out of control when you are frightened.

Fear about exams

A common fear is that of failure in exams. This is because students don't know what is going to happen in the future, and imagine things that could go wrong. Fears can therefore lead to anxiety and worries.

Here are some suggestions on how to deal with fear about exams.

- Practise doing exam papers in timed conditions.
- Talk about your fears to your friends, family and teachers.
- Make sure that you have thoroughly revised and are prepared for the exam.
- Go to the exam room and familiarise yourself with it. Visualise yourself successfully completing the exam in this room.
- Empower yourself by deciding what you could do to help if you do go blank in the exam, such as visualising your textbook, the lesson or your teacher to help you remember the information you need.

DISCUSS

Look at the list above.

1. Which do you think are the best ways of dealing with fears about exams?

2. Are there any other techniques that you find helpful?

Give reasons for your views.

YOUR CHOICE

Strong irrational fears are called phobias. There are many different phobias. Look at the list below of things people are frightened of. Some are fears and some are phobias. Which do you think are which?

- Spiders
- Doing badly in exams
- Heights
- Getting bullied
- Confined spaces (claustrophobia)
- Letting your parents down
- Wide open spaces (agoraphobia)
- Being alone
- The dark
- Getting embarrassed in front of your friends
- Dogs and other large animals
- Snakes
- Deep water
- Public speaking

Dealing with phobias

Often, the way to deal with a phobia is to recognise how your head is thinking about the situation. Usually, our head is imagining all sorts of terrible things that *could* happen.

Some people manage to overcome their phobias by gradually exposing themselves to them more and more. So, a person who is scared of snakes may start off by looking at and touching pictures of snakes. Once they have become comfortable with this, they may go to the zoo and see snakes from a distance and snakes behind glass. Then they may be in the same room as a snake with a zookeeper. Finally, they may feel they are able to touch or even handle a snake.

Steve's story

'I don't like spiders. It doesn't matter whether it's small or big – I just imagine it coming towards me, really fast.

'It got so bad I went to see a counsellor about it. The counsellor asked questions about my phobia. That's when I realised that every time I see a spider, I'm creating a really big picture of it coming towards me in my mind. The image is so big that I want to run away from it. That is why I was scared.

'With the counsellor's help, I've shrunk the image down in my mind to something small. Now I'm not afraid of spiders any more. I don't like them, but I'm able to deal with them, rather than running away in a panic.'

DISCUSS

In groups, discuss the following:

1. What do you think of Steve's story?

2. Is there anything that you are afraid of, and have a big picture of in your head? Can you make it a smaller picture? Does that make a difference to how you feel?

3. What do you think of the idea of gradually exposing yourself to a phobia, so that you become used to it?

4. Which do you think works best – shrinking down the picture in your mind, or gradually exposing yourself to a phobia? Give reasons for your views.

Panic attacks

A panic attack can be a reaction to an extreme fear. This can trigger off the body's 'fight, flight or freeze' response, which used to be a survival strategy for humans. We are programmed to react in one of three ways in a dangerous situation, from our past as hunter gatherers. We may prepare to fight or to run (flight), so our body pumps us full of adrenaline for both of these things. Our heart beats faster and our breathing becomes shallower. Thinking logically becomes more difficult. The third option is to freeze and stay still, until the danger has passed.

In a panic attack, you stop thinking rationally. Your breathing becomes shallow, and it can be difficult to breathe. Your heart may feel like it is pounding in your chest – heavy and fast. You may become light headed.

After a panic attack or feeling frightened

After feeling frightened or having a panic attack, you can learn from the experience. There are several things you can do.

- If you feel able to, you could talk through the panic attack with someone whom you trust and feel safe with. Avoid remembering it directly, but instead imagine seeing yourself, in black and white, some distance away having the panic attack, with a bubble around you to protect yourself from the feelings you had.

- From a safe emotional distance, describe what started the attack.

- Think about what would help you to avoid feeling like this in the future.

- What helped to bring you out of the panic attack?

Remember, a panic attack can feel very strong. If you or somebody you know has panic attacks on a regular basis, particularly if they are connected to a past event, seek the advice of a doctor or a counsellor who can help you deal with them.

Fear as fun

A final word on fear is that it can be fun. Some people like being scared and enjoy the rush of adrenaline that comes from being frightened. This is why we read or tell each other ghost stories, watch scary movies, and go on rollercoasters at a funfair.

DISCUSS

Do you like being scared for fun? What do you do?

RESEARCH

Use the internet to research the best advice for dealing with a panic attack. Then make a poster, using your research, to advise students how to deal with a panic attack.

12.1 Signs of stress

Stress is the body's way of reacting to a situation. This could be a challenge, a threat or some sort of barrier that exists.

There are many different signs of stress. These can be mental, physical or emotional.

Sometimes the type of language people use reveals that they are under stress, using phrases like, 'I feel tense' or, 'I just can't relax'.

The mental signs of stress

Mental signs of stress include:

- being unable to concentrate
- avoiding big crowds and loud noises
- making silly mistakes with work
- constantly remembering a stressful situation
- doing things unconsciously
- having gaps in memories of what has happened
- having a very critical or negative attitude towards yourself or in general
- confusion about what is happening.

DISCUSS

1. What do people look like when they are stressed? Draw a picture of a stressed person. There can be no words – only pictures, and you must complete this activity on your own, in silence.

   Then compare your pictures as a group, with other people trying to guess what different parts of your picture represent.

2. What sort of words do people use when they are stressed?

3. How do people act when they are stressed?

4. Do you recognise signs of stress in anyone you know?

Physical signs of stress

There are many different physical signs of stress. Stress uses up the body's energy more quickly.

For some people this can lead to feeling tired all the time. Other people may have too much energy, and be unable to sit still when they are stressed, only feeling tired much later.

Stress can affect particular parts of the body differently, for example causing stiff or aching muscles, particularly in the neck and back, and headaches. Stress can also affect the digestive system, including causing changes in appetite, such as wanting to binge eat, or not wanting to eat at all, or only to eat certain types of food, such as junk food to get a quick sugar rush.

Stress can affect us in other ways, including shaking hands, sweaty palms or a dry mouth. It can also lead to an increased heart rate – where our heart feels like its beating faster or harder. Stress can also affect our breathing, making it faster and shallower, as our body tries to move into a fight or flight response, as discussed in Unit 11.3.

Finally, stress can affect our sleep. This can include being unable to get to sleep, oversleeping the next morning or waking up in the middle of the night.

Johnny's story

'What gets me stressed is exams and tests. I'm fine normally in class, but put me in a test and it's like I can't concentrate. I make silly spelling mistakes, get confused and misread the question. Afterwards I put myself down and tell myself I'm useless at exams, because I always get low scores. It becomes the one thing I focus on.

'For my older sister Karen, it's not exams that stress her, but dogs. She was bitten by one when she was young. She says she's forgotten most of the details, but it happened in the centre of town when it was very busy, and she doesn't like large crowds now. I've noticed that when we get to the centre of town she always crosses the street to avoid where it happened.'

YOUR CHOICE

Look at the list of physical stress symptoms. Match them to the solutions given.

Symptoms	Solutions
1. Having a dry mouth	A. Having a healthy snack to hand, like a banana
2. Wanting to binge eat	B. Taking a long hot bath to relax your muscles
3. Not wanting to eat at all	C. Setting an alarm
4. Not being able to get to sleep	D. Taking a break in an activity, for example by going the toilet
5. Waking up in the middle of the night	E. Keeping a food diary, including one or two small snacks each day
6. Oversleeping next morning	F. Breathing out more than breathing in, to slow down your heart rate
7. Tense muscles in your neck and back	G. Making sure you have regular drinks of water
8. Having too much energy	H. Having an early night with a book
9. Feeling tired all the time	I. Exercising so you are tired and will sleep through the night
10. Breathing too hard and too fast	J. Making sure you have plenty of vitamin C and food that will give you energy
11. Feeling like your heart is pounding and thumping in your chest	K. Doing slow balanced breathing – in and out for a count of six

Is there anything else you can think of doing to deal with these symptoms?

HAVE A GO

1. Think about Johnny and Karen's stories.

   - Which one is suffering from symptoms of stress?

   - What do you think can be done to help each of them?

2. Karen's symptoms are a reaction to a past situation. In extreme cases this is called post-traumatic stress disorder, or PTSD. Research PTSD and what can be done to help those who suffer from it.

The emotional signs of stress

There are many different emotional signs of stress. Below is a list of the most common.

- Having a short temper
- Being impatient with people
- Crying for no real reason at all
- Irritability with the world
- Being unable to deal with other people
- Feeling negative for no reason
- Constantly worrying about things
- Being oversensitive to things that don't usually bother you
- Finding it difficult to manage strong emotions like anger
- Feeling like you never get a break
- Feeling emotionally drained

YOUR CHOICE

1. Rank the emotional signs of stress in order of the most serious to the least, in your opinion.

2. Then discuss what someone who has each of these signs of stress could do to help manage their feelings. Give reasons for your views.

12.2 What stresses you?

Stress is part of how human beings have evolved. It helps us in an emergency, causing the fight or flight response discussed earlier. The right amount of stress is actually a good thing.

Pros and cons of stress

Without any stress, we would be very relaxed towards our exams, for example, and wouldn't do much revision. In the exam, we wouldn't perform at our best because the adrenaline that helps our brains to concentrate and perform well wouldn't be released. Afterwards, we wouldn't be concerned about the consequences of passing or failing.

While stress can be useful in some situations, like in a running race or an emergency, too much stress, or stress in the wrong situation, can be harmful. The diagram shows how the right amount of stress can be helpful, but too much can cause problems.

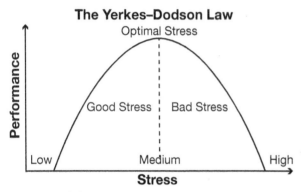

The Yerkes–Dodson Law

Because of this, it is important to recognise what causes stress. This can be a situation you find yourself in or a person you find it stressful to deal/be with.

YOUR CHOICE

1. Look at the list of top ten stressful situations. Rank them in order of the most stressful to the least stressful. Then compare your answers with a partner. Give reasons for your views.

2. Now discuss with your partner what other situations you think would stress you. Give reasons for your views.

Sometimes a person will stress you.

3. Look at the list of people below. Rank them in order from who causes you the most stress to who causes you the least stress.

4. Compare your answers with a friend. Give reasons for your views.

Top ten people that can cause you stress

- Teachers
- Best friend
- Peer group
- Siblings
- Strangers
- Parents
- People who criticise you on social media
- Members of the same sex
- Members of the opposite sex
- Yourself

Top ten stressful situations

- Being late
- Public speaking
- Exams
- Homework
- Sports team trials
- Being on your own
- Being in a large crowd
- Being with people you don't know
- Being with animals
- Peer pressure

Our stress reservoir

Our bodies are like a reservoir – they can store up stress over time in the same way that they can store up anger. It's important to make sure that your stress isn't building up too much. You need to give stress an outlet, to make sure that you get rid of it. Otherwise, if you already have a lot of stress in you, a small amount more can make you snap.

Top ways to avoid stress

- Get half an hour's light exercise every day, such as walking or running. It is important to get any excess adrenaline out of your body.

- Meditate for a short amount of time each day – first thing in the morning and last thing at night.

- Eat healthily.

- Plan your day so that it has regular breaks in it, so you have time to yourself.

- Have at least one close person, such as a friend, parent, carer, grandparent, sibling or cousin to whom you can talk about anything.

- Have at least one day off work or school work every week.

- Go out at least one evening a week.

- Have at least one hobby that you enjoy that you do each week.

- Read a good book for half an hour each day to relax.

YOUR CHOICE

Look at the top ways of avoiding stress.

1. Rank them in order of your personal preference from best to worst.

2. Then discuss your list with a partner. Which ways work best for you and why?

FOMO: the fear of missing out – Becca's story

'I signed onto Instagram when I was 13. At first it was OK: I would use it to post photos of myself and see photos of my friends. But gradually I spent more and more time on the app. I became obsessed with looking good, with what my friends thought of my latest photos, and with looking at other people's perfect lives. It got to the point that I was checking Instagram all the time – so much so that my school work was suffering. My friends noticed that I wasn't paying attention to them – I was always looking at my phone.

'Eventually, my dad became concerned, and we talked the whole thing out. I knew in my gut what I was doing wasn't healthy. My heart just wanted to be liked, but my head kept telling me that I was going to miss out. Eventually I realised that my friends like me for just being myself. Now I spend more time with them in real life and have agreed to limit myself to using social media for only an hour a day. That might sound extreme to some people, but I'm a lot happier now.'

DISCUSS

In groups, discuss Becca's story.

1. What do you think 'fear of missing out' means?

2. Do you ever experience fear of missing out because of social media? How does this make you feel?

3. What could you do to avoid this?

WRITE

Create a short social media post, aimed at people the same age as you, on how to avoid stress in the first place.

1. Create a draft of your post in pairs.
   - What social media app will you use?
   - What is the main aim of your post?
   - What will you include?

2. Share your post in groups, and then with the class.
   - Which post do you think is the best? Why?

12.3 Coping with stress

Coping with stress is very important, as stress can lead to real problems with our health.

The long-term effects of stress

Apart from the issues that we've already looked at, stress can lead to a range of problems. Physically, stress can limit children's growth, cause heart disease and lower the immune system. Mentally and emotionally, stress can lead to depression, delusions or anxiety. There is a strong link between stress and illness. Chronic stress is classed as a long-term medical condition.

Because stress affects different people in different ways, every person has a different way of dealing with their stress.

RESEARCH

Developing your emotional resilience can help you to reduce the impact of stress on your life. Do some research on the internet to find out more about emotional resilience and how you can develop yours.

YOUR CHOICE

Look at the list below of ways people deal with their stress.

1. Which do you think would work for you? Which wouldn't be so good for you?

2. Rank them in order from most helpful to least helpful.

3. Then compare your answer in groups. Give reasons for your views.

4. What other ways can you think of for reducing stress?

Ways people deal with their stress

- Having a good cry
- Hanging out with close friends
- Going to the gym
- Having a warm shower or bath
- Going for a long walk
- Listening to music
- Overeating until you are too full
- Drinking alcohol or taking drugs
- Avoiding going to school
- Doing the thing that makes you smile the most
- Talking the problem through with a responsible adult
- Getting annoyed with other people
- Talking the problem through with a friend your age
- Consulting with an expert, such as a teacher for education, a doctor for health, or the police for a crime

Caitlin's coping strategies

'I use different strategies to avoid, recognise and deal with stress, depending on what type of stress it is. My biggest one is emotional stress, when I am arguing with people.

'The first thing I do is to avoid argumentative situations. So I don't hassle my parents when I can see they are stressed, or if I'm already feeling stressed. I don't talk about tricky things just before school, when everyone is rushing out, or last thing at night when everyone is tired. I pick my moments.

'Next, I remind myself that sometimes I will disagree with other people. So, if I'm arguing with my brother or my parents and things are going round in circles I will stop and take a break if I feel myself getting stressed or can see that the other person is. It's better to take a break and work things out later rather than winding each other up.

'Finally, I don't hold on to things. If I've had an argument, I will go out for a run to get the stress out of my body physically. I'll clear my mind by watching a film, reading a book or listening to some music in my bedroom, to get rid of the mental stress. If it's a bad argument I will talk to another member of my family or my friend Jazz. She's great as she's a calm person to chat to and always gives me good advice.'

DISCUSS

Think about and discuss Caitlin's ways of coping with stress. Which part of her advice do you think is best? Give reasons for your views.

WRITE

1. Write down the answers to these scenarios, to help understand how to deal with stress:

   - When a person I know is stressed about another person, what can I do?

   - When a person I know is in the middle of a stressful situation, what can I do?

   - When a person I know is in the middle of a stressful conversation, what can I do?

   - When a person I know is stressed after an event, what can I do?

   - What a person I know is stressed after a stressful conversation, what can I do?

2. Does the answer to any of these questions change depending on whether it is physical, emotional or mental stress that a person is experiencing?

DISCUSS

1. In pairs or groups, imagine you had to build a mobile app that would help you deal with stress.

   - What features would it have?

   - What would it be able to do?

2. List as much information about your app as possible.

3. Then compare your apps with the rest of the class.

Study skills

One area which students need to develop is that of study skills. This is the ability to study, research, learn and remember information – and avoid stress while doing it. Fortunately, there are a number of very simple things you can do in order to study effectively.

Different ways of studying effectively

'I always find it easier to study in the morning.' Alice, Birmingham

'I study best in the evening.' Dalton, Leeds

'I like studying after school each day.' Tandi, Newcastle.

'I like to break things up into bite-sized chunks.' Natalie, Lincoln

'I like looking at the big picture first.' Simon, Redruth

'I like reading to learn new things – either books or on the internet.' Tom, Huddersfield

'I like watching videos or YouTube clips for new information.' Sasha, Taunton

'I like talking to other people to find out new information.' Ben, Coventry

'I like working on my own to figure things out myself.' Krishnan, Carlisle

DISCUSS

1. In groups, discuss the following statements. Which do you agree with and why?

2. Draw up a list of things that make it easier for you to study.

3. In groups, discuss:

   - what time of day you find best for studying

   - how you like to get new information

   - how you like to digest and think about information.

4. Are there any differences within your group?

5. What have you learned about yourself by thinking about how you study and learn best?

13.1 You and the bank

People need a safe place to keep their money, where they can deposit and withdraw it, and arrange for it to be transferred to another person. They also need somewhere they can go to for financial advice. All of this is done by a bank.

Bank accounts: your questions answered

Q: What is a bank account?

A: This is an arrangement you have with a bank to keep your money there and to withdraw it when you need it.

Q: At what age can I open a bank account?

A: You can't open a bank account on your own until the age of 18. However, you can open one with your parents at any age. Some parents open bank accounts for their children when they are born.

Q: What is a current account?

A: A current account allows you to access your money instantly. Current accounts are useful if you need easy access to your money, such as to pay for the cinema or going out. Because you have instant access to your money, the banks give you very little reward for keeping the money with them. This means the rate of interest will be low to none.

Q: What is the rate of interest?

A: Interest is the reward you get for keeping your money in a bank account. It is calculated using the annual percentage rate, or APR. For example, if you had £100 in a bank account for a year, and the APR was two per cent, at the end of one year you would have £102.

Q: What is a savings account?

A: A savings account is for money that you don't need instantly. You may have to give the bank notice before you withdraw this money. Sometimes this is 3 months or 90 days. Because the bank is able to keep your money for longer, you will usually receive a higher rate of interest for a savings account.

Q: How do banks make money?

A: Once you have stored some money at the bank, the bank can use it to lend out to other people and charge them interest on the loan. So, while you may get two per cent for leaving your money in a bank for a year, the bank may charge a person five per cent to borrow the same amount of money. This means the bank will make at least three per cent every time it lends somebody this money.

Q: What is online banking?

A: Online banking is where you can interact with your bank online. You can make payments or transfer money between accounts (for example, from a current account to a savings account) all online, without ever visiting the bank.

Q: What is a bank card?

A: A bank card is a card that you can use to take money out of a cash machine. You can also use it to pay for things in shops or online.

Q: What is a cash machine?

A: A cash machine, or ATM (automatic teller machine) is a machine from which you can withdraw cash from your bank account and find out what your balance is. You do this by using your PIN (personal identification number) code.

Q: What is my balance?

A: This is the amount of money that is in your account.

Q: What is my PIN code?

A: Your PIN code is a four-digit number that you use when buying goods or taking money out of your account. It is secret and you shouldn't share it with anybody.

Q: What are wireless or contactless payments?

A: A contactless or wireless payment is when you just touch the machine with your card to pay for something and do not need to use your PIN code. The maximum amount you can pay using contactless is £30.

Keeping your bank account safe

In recent years, bank fraud has become more of a problem in the UK. This is when a criminal tries to steal money from your bank account. There are several dos and don'ts to follow, in order to keep the money in your bank account safe:

- Always keep your PIN code safe – never reveal it to anyone.

- Be careful when you are entering your PIN code into a cash machine – make sure that nobody is looking over your shoulder.

- Make sure your PIN code is a secret and is secure. For example, 1234 is not a secure pin. Nor is 0000.

- Criminals have been known to add extra slots onto a machine to read data and a secret pinhole camera to record you entering your PIN code. If a machine looks suspicious, do not use it and report it to the bank or machine operator.

- Keep your card safe. Do not keep it in your back pocket or loose in a bag where it can be easily stolen or fall out.

- Do not let your card out of your sight when you are paying for something. A common trick is to scan the card twice – which means you could end up paying twice for something.

- If your card is lost or stolen, report it immediately as criminals can use your card's contactless feature even without your PIN. If you report it to your bank, it can cancel your card and will usually refund any money that has been stolen.

- Also take precautions with online payments, making sure you keep your password and data safe. Online fraud is the most common type.

RESEARCH

1. Which bank accounts for children and young adults pay the best rate of interest? Research online to find the best deal.

2. What restrictions are there for withdrawing your money from such accounts?

3. Draw a table like the one below to list the different bank accounts available, whether you can access your money instantly or have to give notice, and how much interest they pay.

Type of bank account	Instant access or notice period	How much interest it pays

WRITE

In pairs, design a poster on keeping your bank account safe. Use the internet to add extra points to your poster, along with those mentioned above.

13.2 Saving and borrowing

It is a good idea to save money. Sometimes you will want to save money for a specific reason, such as an expensive video game or a computer. You may be generous and be saving up to buy somebody else a present. Or you may need a piece of equipment to pursue a hobby.

There are many different ways of saving money. Each has their own advantages and disadvantages.

Formal ways of saving

Formal ways of saving include placing your money in a savings account with a bank. With a savings account, you do not always get instant access to your money. Instead, you may have to give notice to your bank that you wish to withdraw your money. This allows the bank to lend your money to other people and charge interest on it while you don't have it, which allows the bank to make greater profits.

However, the upside to this is that the bank will pay you a higher rate of interest than with a current account, which often won't pay any interest at all, or an instant access savings account. So, if you don't need your money instantly, you will make more interest and get more money in the long run.

Premium Bonds

Premium Bonds are a type of saving issued by the government. They don't pay guaranteed interest, but once a month there is a Premium Bond draw, which is like a raffle. If you win on the Premium Bond draw, you can receive from tens to hundreds of thousands of pounds. Premium Bonds are for people who like the element of luck, and at the same time don't mind not receiving interest on their money because there is no risk of losing it.

Informal ways of saving

Informal ways of saving can include saving up your spare change in a jar at home, or letting your parents keep money for you. While this means you will always have the money whenever you want it, you won't be earning any interest on it, unless your parents are being generous to you.

ACTUAL

A friend wants to save up to buy a ticket for a music festival next summer. The tickets go on sale in six months' time and will cost £120. With one of you taking the role of the friend, talk through the informal options for saving and decide which would be the best in this situation.

DISCUSS

Look at the situations below.

1. In each case, which kind of bank account do you think the person needs: a current account, an instant access savings account or a high-interest savings account where they have to give notice to withdraw their money?

2. Or should they save their money informally?

Give reasons for your views.

a) A grandparent wants to save up money to buy their grandchild a big birthday present. However, sometimes in the winter they may need occasionally to use some of the money to pay a heating bill.

b) A young girl is saving money to go to a show-jumping exhibition next summer. However, she uses a little bit of money each week to pay for her riding lessons.

c) A young couple want to save money for their child to go to university. They won't need the money until the child is 18.

d) A young boy wants to save his spare change each week, but likes to use some money to buy sweets on a Saturday as a treat.

e) A teenager wants to save as much money as possible, as quickly as possible, to buy a new computer.

Why would you borrow money?

Sometimes, you may want to borrow money. As a young person, you will not be able to get a credit card (a card where you can spend the money and then pay it back at a high rate of interest) before you are 18. However, you may be able to borrow money from your parents.

It is important when you borrow money that you are able to pay it back. You need to agree with your parents how much you will pay back, and when you need to pay it back. This sum needs to be realistic.

Joshua's story

'I borrowed £60 from my parents to buy a new computer game. I said I would use the money from my paper round, and pay them back at £10 per month, over six months. My problem was that I forgot Christmas was coming up, and I wanted to use the money to buy presents as well. When I told my parents, they were annoyed with me but agreed to give me three extra months to pay the money back. Now I've learned my lesson. If I ever borrow money again in the future, I'll be much more careful.'

Loan sharks

Loan sharks are criminals who go door to door offering to lend people money. However, they charge very high rates of interest. Often, there will be no formal contract for the amount of money lent. This means that loan sharks can charge people what they like and increase the amount of interest or money owed whenever they like. They may use violence and threats when people cannot pay their money on time. You should never borrow money from a loan shark.

WRITE

Imagine you want to borrow some money. Use the questions below to write a plan for how you are going to go about it, giving reasons for your answers.

1. Who would you borrow the money from?

2. How would you go about it?

3. What are the advantages and dangers of borrowing money?

4. How would you plan to pay the money back?

14.1 Laws and the rights of children

Laws are the rules that apply to everyone in the country.

Types of law

There are many different types of law. The most important are statute laws – laws that have been passed by Parliament.

There are also case laws. These are when there is a gap in the law which has been covered by a judge ruling in a legal case in the past. Past legal cases make up case law.

Then there is common law. When a judge finds a gap in the law they may rule on it, in effect creating a new law. This is known as common law.

A gap in the law

A person was injured because a young man was firing an air gun out of a high-rise flat window. The person was hit by an air pellet. There were no laws or previous cases covering air guns in an accident. The judge declared common law and found the man guilty.

There are special laws for people below the age of 18. These are designed to protect young people, who may not understand the impact a decision can have. This doesn't mean young people aren't respected, but that responsible adults may make decisions on their behalf.

YOUR CHOICE

1. In groups, draw a chart.
- Put the ages 10–18 down the left-hand side of the paper.
- On the right-hand side, list the activities you think young people should be able to do at a particular age.
2. Compare your charts in a class discussion, then use the internet to find out what the ages are in the UK for the activities you've listed.

Children in care

In some cases, parents may not be able to look after their children. In the most serious cases, children may be taken into care. This can include living with foster parents, adoptive parents or in a children's home. A care order is made if direct harm is likely to come to you or others by staying with your family.

Tina's story

'My parents split up when I was young. My dad never wanted anything to do with me. He lives in America now. We never hear from him.

'The break-up hit my mum hard, and she started using drugs. When I was six, my mum took an overdose. The police found her and alerted social services.

'Now I live with my foster parents – Toby and Diane. I know they're not my real parents, but it's somewhere stable and safe where they can watch out for me.

'I see my mum once a week. There's a social worker there to make sure all the meetings go OK. My mum is still battling with drugs. One day I hope she'll sort things out. In the meantime, I'm happy with my foster parents.'

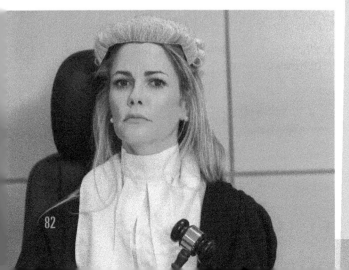

Joe's story

'My parents physically fight. While my dad is much stronger than my mum, my mum's got nails and scratches him. Last time, she made his face bleed. The police got involved. They found out my parents have been stealing to spend money on drink.

'I'm currently in a children's home, with five other kids. It's all right. I know it's only temporary. I don't want to live here with other kids. I want a place of my own with someone who cares for me.'

DISCUSS

Think about Tina's and Joe's stories.

What do you learn from them about the circumstances that can lead to children living apart from their biological parents?

Discipline and smacking

Sometimes children misbehave, and parents may need to use discipline to help them make better decisions. This discipline might involve removing pocket money or restricting access to phones, computers or the internet. In some cases, parents use physical force.

The Children's Act of 2004 allows smacking in cases of 'reasonable punishment' for children. However, the law is unclear as it to what a 'reasonable punishment' is. It is clear, however, that leaving a permanent mark on a child, such as a bruise, is excessive force and against the law.

Scotland and Wales have removed the exemption for smacking to be used as reasonable punishment. However, England is planning to keep the defence of 'reasonable punishment'.

RESEARCH

Use a website recommended by your teacher to do further research on the change to the law in Scotland and Wales.

WRITE

Write a paragraph answering this question: 'Is the current English law about smacking children fair in your opinion?'.

You and the law in school

All children between the ages of 5 and 18 should be in full-time education or training. You can apply to the school for permission to go on holiday in term time, but the school does not have to grant permission. If you miss school without permission, your parents can be fined for breaking the law.

In 2015, Jon Platt from the Isle of Wight took his daughter out of school in term time to go to Florida. He was fined £120 for doing so. Mr Platt complained, and took his case through the legal system in the UK, arguing that his daughter had good attendance up to then. He also argued he should be able to decide what was best for his daughter.

In 2018, the UK Supreme Court said Mr Platt had been in the wrong. This confirmed a piece of case law – that parents can be fined if they do not make sure that their children attend school regularly.

DISCUSS

Should adults be allowed to take their children on holiday in term time, due to high holiday prices in the school holidays? Or should they obey the law as it stands? Can you think of any circumstances which would justify taking a child out of school? Give reasons for your views.

14.2 You and the police

The police force is an organisation that maintains law and order in the country and detects and prevents crime.

The police have several different roles in the UK. First, they are there to protect people and their property. This can include intervening by arresting people to stop fights, or to prevent people from being hurt or property from being damaged.

This is linked to their second function of keeping public order. A law called 'keeping the peace' allows the police to arrest somebody who is creating trouble – it is a very broad but useful power as it is not too specific.

The third role of the police is to prevent and detect crime. If people are caught breaking the law or persist in behaviour that is illegal, the police can arrest them and take them to a police station.

The police also help people who need information or are in trouble.

Attitudes towards the police

'You can go to the police when you need help. I feel I can rely on them.' Zac, Winchester

'Nobody trusts the police on my estate. They're always stopping the young lads who live there – but never the kids from the expensive flats across the road.' Liza, Accrington

'The police are racist – they always suspect Black and Asian people first over White people.' Akram, London

'The media only report on the police when they make mistakes, and not the good work that they do.' Ian, Yeovil

'Teenagers don't like the police, because the police don't like teenagers.' Nisha, Huddersfield

'The police have a difficult job to do, and they do it to the best of their ability.' Joanne, Folkestone

DISCUSS

In groups, discuss what you think of the police.

1. Which of the statements above do you agree with, and why?

2. Have you or has anyone you know had any contact with the police? Were the police helpful or unhelpful in this situation?

3. Because of the increase in knife crime in 2018-19, should police powers of stop and search be extended to allow the police to carry out random searches of young people?

Fact check

The police are allowed to stop and search you if they suspect you of having committed or being about to commit a crime. If they have reasonable grounds to suspect you of carrying illegal drugs, a weapon such as a knife or stolen property, they may ask you for your name and address, check inside your bag or ask you to take off your outer clothing so they can search you.

In 2016–17, there were almost 300 000 stop and searches by the police, the equivalent of five stop and searches for every 1000 people in the UK. This was down from 23 searches per 1000 people in 2009–10.

However, in 2016–17, there were four stop and searches per 1000 White people and 29 per 1000 Black people. In other words, you were more than seven times more likely to be stopped and searched if you were Black than if you were White.

Statistics from the Home Office, May 2018

ID cards

Before 2010, it was proposed by the Labour Government that we should all carry ID cards. Labour argued that this would help combat crime. ID cards are common in other countries, such as France and Poland.

However, civil liberties groups campaigned against this. They argued that in the UK we have a long history of a right to privacy. Worse still in their opinion, the police would then be able to stop anyone without good reason to ask to see their identity card. This would mean that the stop and search figures would go up.

When the Coalition Government of the Conservatives and Liberal Democrats took power in 2010, one of the first things they agreed on was their opposition to ID cards. The proposal was scrapped in the Freedom Act of 2011.

WRITE

Bullet-point an argument for or against the introduction of ID cards.

Terrorism

As part of their role to uphold the law and keep the public safe, the police have to combat terrorism. The Metropolitan Police, based in Greater London, leads in this role. However, all police forces have a counter-terrorism role. This includes preventing people from becoming radicalised and supporting terrorist groups. It also includes undercover work to discover and prevent terrorist plots. The police also respond to suspected terrorist incidents, such as bomb threats.

The job of the police can be difficult. The threat of terrorism has sometimes led to tension and mistrust between the police and particular communities. For example, because of the threat of Islamist terrorism, the police have had more contact with Muslim communities to prevent this.

There is also the growing problem of extreme-right terrorism. This means the police have to investigate and liaise with a wide range of people to prevent terrorism.

RESEARCH

Using the GOV.UK website, research how many terrorist plots the police have stopped over the last three years.

1. Are the numbers going up or down?

2. What sorts of plots are the police stopping?

3. Do any of the figures surprise you?

Give reasons for your views.

Arrests

If you have committed a major offence, such as assaulting somebody, the police have the power to arrest you. However, if you have committed only a minor offence, such as not paying for a train ticket, the police may just take your name and address. Later you may get a summons from court, where a magistrate may force you to pay the fine.

The police have the power to keep you under arrest for a maximum of 24 hours, unless you are arrested under the Terrorism Act, or are under suspicion for a serious offence such as murder. After that, you must be charged with an offence or let go.

YOUR CHOICE

Think about the following offences:
- vandalism
- carrying a knife
- refusing to give your name and address to a police officer
- joyriding in a car or stolen vehicle
- possession of drugs with intent to supply
- robbery
- causing criminal damage
- cyberbullying
- inciting racial hatred.

1. For which ones do you think you can be arrested?

2. For which ones might you only get a court summons?

15.1 Democracy and voting

The word democracy means 'people power' or government by the people. This means that power is meant to be controlled by ordinary people. The United Kingdom is a democracy.

There are two types of democracy: first, direct democracy and secondly, representative democracy.

Representative democracy

Representative democracy is also known as indirect democracy. Imagine you were deciding on where your year group would go on a school trip. Each class within the year group will elect one representative by holding a class vote. The winning candidates from each class (those with the highest number of the votes) become your representatives and make the decision about the school trip. So you don't make the decision yourselves. Instead, the people you elect as your representatives do. Hence, this is known as indirect democracy.

This is the most common form of democracy used around the world today, including in the UK, across the European Union, Canada, the USA and many other countries. The largest democracy in the world is India.

In a representative democracy, people who hold similar views come together to form a political party. There are many different political parties in the United Kingdom, including parties for Scotland, Wales and Northern Ireland. The two main political parties in England are the Conservatives, who were the party in government early in 2023, and Labour, who were the opposition party.

In the UK, we use representative democracy to elect several different levels of government. We elect Members of Parliament (MPs) to the House of Commons, also known as the lower chamber. In 2019, there were 650 MPs, each representing one constituency (area) of about 100 000 people, of whom around 70 000 are voting aged adults over 18.

However, constituencies vary in size, so to make things fairer, it is proposed to make the constituencies bigger, so that there are only 600 of them with a more equal number of people in each.

Unlike many other countries, we don't elect members of our upper chamber, the House of Lords. Instead, the majority of the members are appointed.

Scotland and Wales have their own Parliaments, and Northern Ireland and London have their own Assemblies.

The Scottish Parliament

1. Find out how people are appointed to the House of Lords and decide for yourself whether the United Kingdom is actually a democracy if we can't vote for the Lords.

2. Research the Scottish and Welsh parliaments, and the Northern Irish and London Assemblies:
   - What powers does each have?
   - How do they elect their members?
   - What do they do?

Plan an election for a class representative.

- How are you going to run the election?
- Using the internet, research and decide what electoral system you will use.

Votes at 16

Some people believe that the age at which you can vote (18) is too high. Groups like Unlock Democracy believe that the voting age should be lowered to 16. This is the policy of the Liberal Democrats and is something that has been discussed in the Labour Party.

However, the Conservative Party believes that the voting age is correct, and should remain at 18. In the Scottish independence referendum in 2014, the Scottish Government allowed 16- and 17-year-olds to vote on whether Scotland should become an independent country.

Look at the following statements. Which ones do you most agree with? Give reasons for your views.

'You can join the army when you are 16, so I don't see why you can't vote at 16.'
Louis, Manchester

'Young people's secondary education finishes at 18, so that's when you should be able to vote.'
Jess, Bournemouth

'Young people are too immature to vote at 16; 18 is much better.'
Ellie, Oxford

'If you pay tax on money you earn, you ought to be able to say how that money is spent by voting.'
Jake, Chesterfield

'I think you should be able to vote in local elections at 16, and national elections at 18, because they are going to determine our future.'
Margda, Colchester

Direct democracy

Direct democracy is when everyone comes together to make a decision that directly affects them. For example, in the scenario where you are deciding where to go for your class trip, everyone in the class has a vote on where to go rather than delegating it to a representative to decide. This is direct democracy.

Direct democracy was first invented in Athens, in ancient Greece. It was the first example of a democracy because the people were making the decisions for themselves directly. It wasn't much of a democracy, though, as women, slaves and children had no say in what was going on.

We sometimes use direct democracy for important decisions. When we do this it is known as a referendum. Between 1975 and 2023, there have only be three national referenda across UK as a whole. The first was in 1975, to decide whether to remain in the European Economic Community, the forerunner of the European Union. The answer was 'Yes'. The second was to decide whether or not to change the way we vote in the UK from our current system to a system known as the alternative vote. The answer was 'No'.

The last referendum was the one you have probably heard about – the referendum on whether or not to leave the European Union. In June 2016, 52 per cent of the people voting in the UK voted to leave the EU, while 48 per cent voted to remain in it.

Some countries like Switzerland use direct democracy for some decisions. Research how referenda are used in Switzerland, and how widespread this is. Write a short report of two to three paragraphs explaining what you find out.

15.2 You and human rights

A human right is something to which every person is entitled.

There are a whole range of different human rights in the UK. Some are for adults, such as the right to vote and the right to have children. Children also have special rights, such as the right to play.

There are three main sources of human rights in the UK: the Universal Declaration of Human Rights, the European Convention on Human Rights and the European Charter of Fundamental Rights. There is also the United Nations Convention on the Rights of the Child, which is part of the Universal Declaration of Human Rights.

The European Convention on Human Rights, and the 1998 Human Rights Act

This was created in 1953. The idea was to avoid the human rights abuses that had occurred in the Second World War under the Nazis. A group of countries, called the Council of Europe, came together to sign the document. Today the Council of Europe includes almost all the countries of Europe, including those outside the European Union (such as Norway and Switzerland), as well as Russia.

The European Convention includes the following important rights:

- freedom of expression
- freedom of movement
- the right to life
- freedom from slavery
- freedom from torture.

These rights are upheld by the European Court of Human Rights, which is based in Strasbourg. In 1998, the UK Government decided to make the European Convention of Human Rights part of British Law. This became the 1998 Human Rights Act.

RESEARCH

Using the internet, research what is included in one of the following rights:

- freedom of expression
- freedom of movement
- the right to life.

DISCUSS

In groups, discuss which of the above rights you think are the most important. Give reasons for your views.

The Universal Declaration of Human Rights

This was created in 1948. Unlike the European Convention, the Universal Declaration is not legally binding. In other words, countries who have signed the declaration take its advice as a recommendation, rather than something that they are forced to do. For example, the Universal Declaration of Human Rights includes the right to life, but countries like the USA and China still have the death penalty. The UN does not approve, but the countries are not legally forced to change their laws.

The Universal Declaration is also wider than the European Declaration. It includes social rights, such as:

Article 17 – The right to own property

Article 23 – The right to work

Article 26 – The right to a free education.

Critics of the Universal Declaration argue that some of the articles include things that are not rights. Supporters of the Universal Declaration disagree. Instead they argue that there is a wide list of rights that should apply to people in order for them to be able to live their lives. These include the right to:

- housing
- a job
- a minimum wage.
- food and clean water
- clothing

Look at the 30 rights in the Universal Declaration of Human Rights.

1. Which do you think should be part of British law, and legally binding? Which do you think should we be forced to do as a society?

2. Which do you think we should not?

Give reasons for your views.

The European Charter of Fundamental Rights

This is a set of rights passed by countries in the European Union in 2000. It became part of European Law in 2009. It includes extra rights, such as the right to improved data protection. It also includes the right to genetic integrity, which means you have a right to say what happens to any materials a hospital or scientist may take from your body.

In groups of three, each pick one document to research – the Universal Declaration of Human Rights, the European Convention on Human Rights and the European Charter of Fundamental Rights. Then compare them. How much do the documents overlap with each other?

The UN Convention on the Rights of the Child

This was passed in 1989. In order for it to come into effect, 20 countries had to sign it. The UK signed in 1990, and the Convention took effect in 1992. It has several key areas which especially apply to children:

Participation

Children have the freedom to express their opinions on any issue that affects them. This led the UK Government to realise that children weren't being heard in the UK political system, as only people aged 18 and over can vote. As a result, the UK Youth Parliament was set up in 2000 to represent young people between the ages of 11 and 18 in the UK.

Survival rights

These include the basic necessities to survive, such as food, clean water, clothing and housing. In particular, the UN has campaigned around the world on the issue of clean water for children. Some children's education suffers in some countries because they spend over four hours walking over 10 miles to and from their houses just to get water, which sometimes isn't even clean.

Developmental rights

These rights include the right to an education up to the end of secondary school or 18. As part of this, there is freedom of expression, which includes freedom of speech, and freedom of religion. There is also a unique right for children – the right to play, which the UN believes is important.

Protection rights

These rights exist to protect children and make sure all their other rights within the convention are protected. They include freedom from slavery and exploitation, and the right to remain as part of a family.

In pairs, look at the UN Convention on the Rights of the Child.

1. Which rights do you think are the most important? Choose ten and rank them in order of importance.

2. Then compare your list with another pair.

Give reasons for your views.

15.3 Pressure groups

A pressure group is a group of people who seek to influence government policies and the views of other citizens.

Unlike a political party, pressure groups do not seek power. Instead, they try to change the government's mind on a particular issue, or a set of issues.

Single-issue groups

There are many different types of pressure group. Some focus on a single issue. For example, Passport for Pets campaigned for the introduction of microchip passports for pets. This was so pets from outside the UK didn't have to go through long quarantines if they had a Pet Passport. The campaign was successful in 2000 so this group has now disbanded. Such groups are known as issue or cause groups. They are often quite local because they have such a tight focus. Anyone can join this type of pressure group.

There are also issue groups that focus on a set of interconnected issues. For example, Greenpeace and Friends of the Earth both campaign on a range of connected environmental issues. CND (the Campaign for Nuclear Disarmament) campaigns against nuclear weapons, but also on other connected issues such as the arms trade. The RSPB (the Royal Society for the Protection of Birds) is one of the largest pressure groups in the UK with over 1 million members. It campaigns on any issue that effects the health and safety of birds. Again, anyone can join this group.

RESEARCH

Research a pressure group on an issue that interests you. What issue is it campaigning on? Has it been successful?

Sectional groups

This sort of group represents a particular section of society. It includes all trade unions, which represent the interests of their members in the workplace. An example is the National Education Union, which represents teachers. There is also UNISON, which represents a wide range of people working in the public sector.

Other sectional groups represent a particular section of society. The Confederation of British Industry (CBI) is made up of the vast majority of leading businesses in the UK. It is considered to be the most influential sectional group in the UK as it has very close links with government.

Sometimes a pressure group won't fit into either category easily. The Countryside Alliance is free for anyone to join, and campaigns on issues that affect the countryside. This includes making fox hunting legal again. However, the Countryside Alliance acts also like a sectional group, as it is made up of many people who work in the countryside, like farmers, and so represents their interests.

Campaign methods

There is a wide variety of campaign methods that pressure groups use to persuade government to agree with them. Here are some of them.

Lobbying

Lobbying is when a representative of a pressure group meets directly with a decision maker in government, to persuade them to their point of view. This is the most effective campaign method pressure groups can use. The CBI describes itself as the UK's premier lobbying organisation.

However, there is a problem with lobbying in that other citizens cannot see what is going on, or who has met whom and discussed what. This has led to calls for lobbying to be more transparent in the UK.

Joint committees

Some pressure groups join an official government committee in order to influence government policy. For example, the National Farmers Union sits on various agriculture committees. It aims to influence government policy and inform the government of what is happening among its members.

Reports

Sometimes a pressure group will produce a joint report with government or contribute to a government report. This can be helpful if the pressure group has extra information that the government doesn't have.

However, the problem with joint committees and reports is that they may prevent pressure groups from being independent. What happens when the government doesn't act in the way the pressure group wants?

Petitions

A petition is one way of showing the strength of feeling the public has on an issue. Petitions can be officially sent to Parliament. If a petition receives more than 10 000 signatures within six months, the government has to respond to it. If a petition receives more than 100 000 signatures, MPs decide whether or not to hold a debate on the issue in Parliament.

Marches

Marches are used by pressure groups to influence the government by creating media pressure. In October 2018, 670 000 people marched through London to campaign against Brexit. This received a lot of media coverage at the time, but didn't change the government's mind.

Civil disobedience

Civil disobedience is when a person breaks the law to draw attention to their issue or cause and influence the general public. However, this is done by avoiding harm to anyone. Examples include CND campaigners blocking the road outside the Faslane Nuclear Base in Scotland, to protest against nuclear weapons.

Direct action

Direct action directly affects the issue a group is campaigning on. The group Plane Stupid wants to stop people flying as it pollutes the air with climate-changing gases. Because the government won't ban plane flights, Plane Stupid take direct action by blocking runways and occupying check-in terminals in order to stop planes from flying.

Terrorism

In rare cases, some pressure groups have used extreme methods, including acts of terrorism, to advance their views. Terrorism involves the use of violence and terror to stop people from doing something. Terrorists may break the law in the name of their cause.

DISCUSS

1. What other campaign methods can you think of? For example, how do pressure groups use social media or publicity stunts to get their message across?

2. Which campaign methods do you think are the most effective within a democratic society? For example, do you read adverts in online newspapers? Would you pay attention to protestors sitting outside your favourite shop? Would you engage with a social media post if it was endorsed by a celebrity?

Give reasons for your views.

RESEARCH

1. Pick a campaign method and write a short report, two to three paragraphs long, of an example of how it has been used recently by a pressure group.

2. What is the main difference between a pressure group and a political party?

15.4 Blood, organ and stem cell donation

Advances in medicine mean that lives can be saved and improved in many ways. But advances in medicine and scientific research raise moral questions – such as what should happen to a person's body when they die?

Blood donation

Blood transfusions are necessary in many medical situations. For example, if someone has an accident and loses blood through an injury, the blood needs to be replaced. Women who have complications during childbirth may lose blood, and people with certain diseases also need blood transfusions. Blood is transferred into a person's body through their veins.

In order for doctors to have the blood they need to save lives, people donate their blood to be stored in blood banks. You have to be over the age of 17 to give blood. It is a painless and safe procedure.

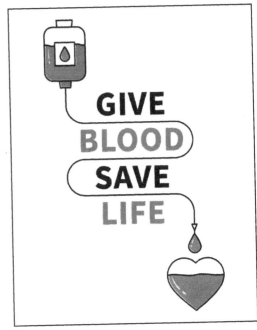

Organ donation and assumed consent

Organ donation is the process of transplanting one person's organs into another person's body in order to save their life. Some organs, such as kidneys, can be donated by a living person. Others, such as a heart or the cornea from an eye, can only be donated when the donor dies.

In the UK, there are about 6 000 people waiting for an organ transplant. Over 400 people die in the UK each year waiting for an organ transplant.

Different parts of the UK have different laws about organ donation. In the past a person has had to 'opt in', in other words to register as an organ donor before their death, for doctors to be allowed to use their organs for transplants. In 2015, the Welsh Government changed the law to an 'opt out' system to try to increase the number of organs available for donation. This means that it is assumed that you agree to your organs being used for transplants when you die, unless you make it clear beforehand that you do not want this.

Whether the system is 'opt in' or 'opt out', the donor's relatives sometimes object to the organ donation and doctors are not able to use the organs. If someone wants their organs to be used after their death it is important that they let their family know their wishes.

The system in Wales has been a success. Between 2015 and 2017, the number of people donating organs after death has risen by 10%. Between 2015 and 2016, the number of people waiting for an organ transplant in Wales fell by 38%. More lives are being saved, due to this simple change in the system.

As a result, the British Government passed a bill in early 2019 to change the law in England, and in 2020 the system will change to one of assumed consent, so you will have to opt out if you don't want your organs to be donated.

In early 2019, the Scottish Government is considering similar proposals.

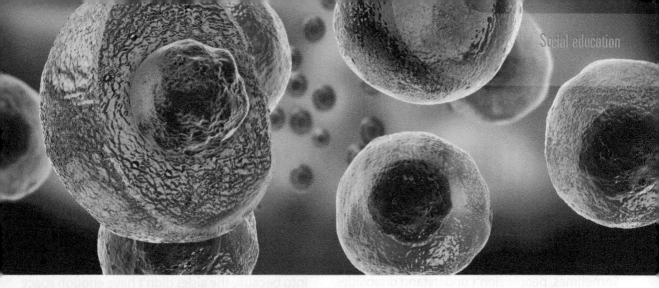

RESEARCH

1. Find out more about blood donation on the 'Give Blood' website.
   - Who can give blood?
   - What happens when you go to give blood?
   - How much blood is taken from one person?
   - What happens to the blood you donate?

2. Do you think you will give blood when you are old enough? Why/why not?

YOUR CHOICE

In pairs, agree and write up a list of three reasons in favour of having an 'opt out' system of organ donation, and three reasons why people might object to this.

Stem cell research

Stem cells are cells that can develop into any other sort of cell. They are the building blocks of the human body. Stem cells are found in embryos (unborn babies) when they are developing in the womb. Other possible sources of stem cells are blood left in the umbilical cord and placenta after a baby is born, and blood stem cells donated by healthy people.

Stem cells are of great interest to scientists. Firstly, because by understanding how stem cells develop into other cells, scientists can understand how many genetic diseases occur. These are diseases passed down from parents to their children. Secondly, scientists are looking into whether stem cells can be used to help treat people with diseases and injuries that are not genetic, such as cancer, spinal injuries,

Alzheimer's disease, diabetes and multiple sclerosis, by injecting a sick person with healthy stem cells.

Further research is needed to find out more about stem cell development, and the best types to use in treatments.

Research controversy

Using stem cells from a living human embryo that has no chance of life is controversial and some people object to it. Until recently, the embryos providing the stem cells were usually those left over from fertility treatments. British law now allows embryos to be created purely for scientific research provided it does one of three things:

1. increases our knowledge about how embryos develop

2. increases our knowledge about serious diseases, including genetic diseases, and how they develop

3. enables knowledge to be used to develop treatments for these serious diseases.

DISCUSS

Think about the following questions and then discuss them in groups:

1. What do you think are the advantages of stem cell research?

2. Why do you think some people object to this type of research?

3. What do you think about the law in Britain about carrying out this type of research?

   Give reasons for your views.

16.1 Disabilities and learning differences

A disability is a substantial or long-term condition that can limit a person's ability to do everyday activities. There are many different sorts of disabilities, including physical, mental and sensory disabilities.

Sometimes, people don't understand disabilities. They think that there are lots of things a person with a disability or learning differences cannot do, when in fact they can do them. Therefore, everyone must be careful to treat people as individuals and with respect and without prejudice.

RESEARCH

Pick one type of disability from the categories below and research what is being done to fight discrimination and prejudice for this particular type of disability. Write up your findings in a report of two to three paragraphs.

Physical disabilities

Physical disabilities are often visible, such as when someone uses a wheelchair. However, just because a person does not use a wheelchair, it does not mean that they can walk long distances. Similarly, just because a person does use a wheelchair, it does not mean they cannot walk at all.

Jamal's story

'I broke my back playing rugby when I was 13. I spent six months in a wheelchair, and then gradually learned to walk. I was lucky: I recovered. However, it was a really eye-opening experience.

'People would look at me differently, as if they were afraid to touch me because I was in a wheelchair. Which is rubbish and discriminatory – I'm still the same person I was before.

'At first things were really negative. I got sick of the indirect discrimination. It isn't just about steps and ramps – there were some shops I couldn't go into because the aisles didn't have enough space to fit my wheelchair into.

'Things got better when my back had healed up enough for me to join the wheelchair basketball team. That was great fun. Those guys really go up against each other and aren't afraid to crash into one another.

'Now I can walk again, and I'm learning to run again. I campaign on disabled issues to make sure people are aware of what they can do for those with disabilities.'

DISCUSS

In groups, discuss the following:

1. What do you learn from Jamal's story?
2. What is the problem with discrimination?
3. What do you think is meant by the phrase 'indirect discrimination'?
4. What do you think can be done to combat this?

WRITE

Imagine you were designing a school.

1. List all the physical disabilities and learning differences you can think of.
2. Then think about all the features that you need to incorporate in your design for the new school.
3. Think also about the accessibility of your school. What would you include in your design to help with this? Give reasons for your views.

Learning differences

Learning differences include a wide range of conditions that can prevent a student from fully accessing school and the subjects being studied. For example, some people have a problem processing certain types of information. This can include dyslexia, where a person has a problem spelling and reading, or dyscalculia, where a person has a problem with numbers. It can also include processing difficulties, such as taking a long time to learn something. There is no 'one size fits all' definition as individual diagnoses will vary.

Anna's story

'I'm dyslexic. I find it difficult to spell. And I'm dyspraxic, which means I can be quite clumsy. I often knock things over. I'm also autistic.

'There are many different types of autism. Mine is relatively mild – I don't like making eye contact with people, and I hate crowds. I find it difficult to understand where people are coming from emotionally. Sometimes I miss the meaning of jokes.

'At primary school it was difficult. Kids who didn't know better would call me nasty names. I was made to feel stupid because I couldn't spell and I was clumsy.

'Things got much better when I was diagnosed. I didn't realise that neurodivergent people can have different skills and abilities to the average person – who are called neurotypical. I can do great things with numbers. Maths is my favourite subject.

'We discussed getting me a support assistant in class, but I found I didn't need one. Everything is printed for me on green paper. This means the words don't dance around the page – it's much easier to read.

'My friends are good to me. I help them with maths homework. They help me with English. When I'm clumsy, we all just laugh. Laughing is the best medicine.'

DISCUSS

Think about at Anna's story.

1. Is there anything that surprises you?

2. What strategies has Anna used to overcome the difficulties she faces?

3. What else can you think of that would help Anna? Give reasons for your views.

Toby's story

'I find it difficult to take on new information. I have to read something five or ten times before I get it. I write really slowly. In school, I have a learning assistant, Sasha. She's really great. She explains things to me carefully. And she points things out when I make a mistake. My teacher has to remember to slow things down for me. I also need to keep things simple. It's the complex ideas I have trouble with.

'My favourite subject is PE. I really like playing rugby. I'm not the best at it, but it's good to be part of the team, especially when we win.'

DISCUSS

1. What measures have the school put in place to help Toby?

2. What else can you think of that would help Toby at his school? Give reasons for your views.

WRITE

Imagine you were planning a day out in London for a school trip, and Jamal, Anna and Toby were all coming along. What would you do to make the trip enjoyable and a success for all the students, including Jamal, Anna and Toby? Give reasons for your views.

16.2 Dealing with ageism

Ageism is when a person is discriminated against on the grounds of age.

Anyone, of any age, can be discriminated against. Often ageism involves stereotyping. This is when we assume that everyone of a particular group has the same characteristics and behaves in the same way. This can be damaging, as people are individuals.

DISCUSS

In pairs, look at the following list of ageist phrases. What would you do to challenge each statement if you heard someone saying it?

'Nothing mature was ever said by a primary school student.'

'Teenagers are always hanging about on the street causing trouble.'

'Middle-aged people are always busy and have no time for anyone else.'

'Young adults don't know what they want for their future.'

'Pensioners are slow and always forget things.'

'Older people are boring because all they go on about is the past.'

'School kids are lazy because all they do is spend all their time on their phones.'

'All children are noisy by nature.'

'Most people's grandparents are confused.'

Ageism against children and young people

Children and young people are often thought to be inexperienced, over emotional and not aware of what they are doing. However, nothing could be further from the truth.

Sure, young people sometimes don't have the experience that older people have. However, what they lack in experience, they make up for in energy, enthusiasm and imagination. That's why it's important to listen to young people, to respect their views (even if you don't agree with them) and to give them a chance to voice their opinions.

DISCUSS

1. Have you ever experienced ageism against children and young people?
2. What do you think of the advice given at the end of the paragraph above?
3. What else would you add? Give reasons for your views.

Ageism towards older people

How we deal with older people is important, because one day we will become old. With people living longer, what is defined as an old person is changing as well. The compulsory retirement age for people used to be 65, which is when people used to start drawing their state pension. However, with the retirement age going up, being old is now being viewed as above the age of 70, or even beyond this.

There are lots of myths and stereotypes about older people. However, just because something is true for one person, it isn't necessarily true for another.

Busting the myths

In 2017, Gladys Thompson became the oldest person to complete a marathon. This involved running 26 miles. Gladys was 94.

Doris Self was a video gamer. In 1984, on a video game called Twin Galaxies, she beat every other person in the world, scoring 1 112 300 points on Twin Galaxies' Tournament Settings, the most difficult setting for this game. She was 81 at the time.

Minoru Saitu has sailed around the world seven times. Including once at the age of 77.

Mohr Keet is the world's oldest bungee jumper – at 96 he did a 708-foot bungee jump on South Africa's West Cape.

Dr Leila Denmark, in America, was the world's oldest doctor. She was still seeing patients and giving them medicine at the age of 103.

Emeritus Professor Dr Heinz Wenderoth is the oldest person to have completed a doctorate and been awarded a PhD – at the age of 97.

Tamae Watanabe is the oldest person to have climbed Mount Everest, at 73.

In the USA, Lt. Col. James C. Warren became the oldest person to obtain a new flying licence – at the age of 87.

DISCUSS

From the list above, which accomplishment surprises you most? Why?

Dealing with dementia and Alzheimer's

Dementia and Alzheimer's are medical conditions that cause memory loss, leading to confusion and anxiety. For example, as the disease progresses someone with Alzheimer's may recognise you one day and then not recognise you another day.

It is easy to discriminate against a person with dementia or Alzheimer's because they are more vulnerable. Just because a person has problems with their memory doesn't mean that they aren't still a person with feelings and opinions, who wants to make decisions for themselves. As a result, there are several steps that exist to prevent people who have dementia or Alzheimer's from being discriminated against.

Living wills

A living will is a will that a person draws up when they are still alive and capable of making decisions. So a person who has dementia may draw up a living will in the early stages of their condition. It doesn't just specify what happens when you die, it also specifies what happens and how you are to be treated when you are no longer able to make decisions for yourself. This can include whether they would like long-term care at home, or whether they would want to move to a care home, and if so, which one.

Living wills are useful because they grant a person an element of choice for when they are no longer able to make decisions for themselves in the future.

Advocate

An advocate is a person who can act independently on another person's behalf. So an advocate may be legally appointed to act in the best interest of a person with dementia or Alzheimer's when they are no longer able to make decisions for themselves. This might include how their money is spent on their behalf, in order to give the person with dementia or Alzheimer's the best possible quality of care.

DISCUSS

1. What do you think of the ideas of a living will and an advocate?

2. What other things do you think we could do to prevent discrimination against people with dementia or Alzheimer's?

Give reasons for your views.

17.1 GCSE choices

At the age of 12–13, many of you will be choosing some of the subjects you will go on to study for GCSE. You will have to do maths, English and science, and other subjects may be compulsory at your school. These and any extra subjects you choose will help to determine your education beyond 16 and your future career.

Making the right decision

Thinking about good and bad choices you have made in the past can help you to make good choices in the future.

YOUR CHOICE

1. Think about a good choice you have made recently. What was good about it? How do you remember it? How did you feel about this choice at the time? How did you know it was the right choice?

2. Now think about a bad choice that you made. What was bad about it? How do you remember it? How did you feel about this choice at the time? When did you realise it was the wrong choice, and how did you know?

3. Finally, compare the differences between the two choices, how you felt and how you came to each decision. These are the things you should pay the most attention to when making a decision in the future.

Choosing the right subjects

'I didn't realise that every job requires maths and English. I want to be a bricklayer, so I'll need to be able to do maths to work out the number of bricks I need to put into a wall, and the amount of cement I'll need for that number of bricks. And I'm going to need English to read the site safety signs.'

'I want to be an engineer, so maths and physics are essential for me.'

'I hope to be a nurse, so I need maths, English and biology or combined science GCSEs. Then I will have to do A levels so that I can get into university to do a nursing degree.'

'I plan to run my own business, so business studies and ICT are good subjects for me, and I need to do well in my maths and English.'

'I want to be a personal trainer, so I need good grades in PE and biology. If I want to teach, I'll need to go to university, which means A levels or a BTEC in sports science. I've found out that I'll need five GCSES at Grade 4 or above for both of these.'

DISCUSS

Some subjects are required for specific careers. Look at the list of statements above.

- Are there any that surprise you?
- Are there any that apply to you?

Give reasons for your views.

Changing subjects

You may need to change a subject choice. If so, it is better to do it early on, rather than continuing with a subject that you don't like. One way to do this is to check how your heart feels about a subject, how your head thinks about it, and whether your gut can swallow continuing with the subject. In the year before GCSE courses start, you may be able to change your subject choices. In the run up to finalising your GCSE choices, discuss with your teachers which subjects you definitely want to do at GCSE.

Consider the following factors to help you decide.

- Which subjects do you enjoy the most?

- Which subjects are you best at?

- Which subjects are necessary for your future career (if you have one in mind)?

If you're not sure what you want to do as a future career, don't worry at this stage, but talk to your parents, friends and school. The school should be able to offer you some careers advice.

WRITE

Write your answers to the three questions above.

DISCUSS

In pairs, talk about which GCSEs you are going to do, and why you want to do them. Give reasons for your views.

RESEARCH

Pick a career you think you might want to go into. Research what qualifications and experience are required.

Breaking targets into chunks

Sometimes it can be difficult to think about a long-term decision. Do you want to be an accountant, or a nurse, or a bricklayer when you are older? How do you get to that career in the long term?

One way of planning for your future is to break what you need to do into chunks or stages.

1. First, think about what your ultimate goal is, say in ten years' time. Imagine that you could do anything – there are no limits.

2. **Then** think about five years' time. What will you be doing? Will you need to pass any A levels, T Levels or BTECs? In what subjects? What grades will you need in order to move on to your ten-year target? Will you need to do an apprenticeship or gain some work experience? If so, what area is this in and with what sort of firm or organisation?

3. Then think about three years' time. What will you be doing at school? What subjects will you be studying? What grades do you need to get to move to your five-year targets?

4. Then think about one year's time. What GCSEs and other qualifications will you be studying for at school? What are your strongest subjects, and how will you excel at them? What are your weakest subjects, and how will you work to improve in these? Where will you need to put in extra effort?

5. Where will you be in each of your subjects in six months' time? What do you need to do to make sure that you can move on to your one-year targets?

WRITE

Write notes in response to your answers to the questions in the flow chart above. Use the headings 'Ten years', 'Five years', 'Three years', 'One year', 'Six months'.

Acknowledgments

The publishers gratefully acknowledge the permission granted to reproduce the copyright material in this book. Every effort has been made to trace copyright holders and to obtain their permission for the use of copyright material. The publishers will gladly receive any information enabling them to rectify any error or omission at the first opportunity.

Images

Key: t = top, b = bottom, l = left, r = right, c = centre.

p7 Malcolm Park editorial/Alamy Stock Photo, p9 trekandshoot/Shutterstock, p11 Palie Massa/Shutterstock, p13 Monkey Business Images/Shutterstock, p14 Iakov Filimonov/Shutterstock, p15 Ian Francis/Shutterstock, p19 Antonio Guillem/Shutterstock, p20 View Apart/Shutterstock, p21 tr MJTH/Shutterstock, p21 br Luxy Images Limited/Alamy Stock Photo, p22 Monkey Business Images/Shutterstock, p26 tl Purple Anvil/Shutterstock, p26 br WhiteJack/Shutterstock, p28 Monkey Business Images/Shutterstock, p29 Image courtesy of Sunderland City Council, p31 Sabphoto/Shutterstock, p32 tr Zhukov Oleg/Shutterstock, p32 bl Jan H Andersen/Shutterstock, p36 Monkey Business Images/Shutterstock, p37 Cernan Elias/Alamy Stock Photo, p38 Marco Iacobucci EPP/Shutterstock, p40 Adam Melnyk/Shutterstock, p41 Couperfield/Shutterstock, p42 Michael McGurk/Alamy Stock Photo, p45 Christian Bertrand/Shutterstock, p47 siamionau pavel/Shutterstock, p48 The infographic on p.70 from Drinkaware, www.drinkaware.co.uk, an independent UK alcohol education charity. Reproduced with permission., p49 Bodnar Taras/Shutterstock, p50 fotoNino/Shutterstock, p52 Yakobchuk Viacheslav/Shutterstock, p56 Lenscap Photography/Shutterstock, p58 sruilk/Shutterstock, p60 Natee Jitthammachai/Shutterstock, p62 Kaspars Grinvalds/Shutterstock, p64 Hero Images Inc./Alamy Stock Photo, p65 chippix/Shutterstock, p66 Cookie Studio/Shutterstock, p69 Prostock-studio/Shutterstock, p70 l Surachai/Shutterstock, p70 r PetlinDmitry/Shutterstock, p73 Tero Vesalainen/Shutterstock, p74 LightField Studios/Shutterstock, p79 SpeedKingz/Shutterstock, p80 Lucie Lang/Shutterstock, p82 wavebreakmedia/Shutterstock, p83 SpeedKingz/Shutterstock, p86 Ulmus Media/Shutterstock, p89 Jayakumar/Shutterstock, p91 Ink Drop/Shutterstock, p92 AlexOrel/Shutterstock, p93 Giovanni Cancemi/Shutterstock, p95 Gideon Ikigai/Shutterstock, p97 Alexei Zinin/Shutterstock, p98 goodluz/Shutterstock.

Texts

We are grateful to the following for permission to reproduce copyright material:

An extract on p.19 from Disrespecting NoBody, PSHE Association and drawn from Crown Prosecution Service (CPS) guidance on consent, Crown © copyright; An extract on p.29 from "Half of young people do not use condoms for sex with new partner" by Tom Barnes, *The Independent*, 15/12/2017, copyright © The Independent, www.independent.co.uk; An extract on p.33 from "At 14, I was excited to get male attention" by Mared, *The Daily Telegraph*, 11/06/2018, copyright © Telegraph Media Group Limited 2018; An extract on p.35 from *TES Online Safety Special Edition*, 13 Oct 2017, https://www.tes.com/teaching-resource/tes-online-safety-special-11751651, copyright © TES. Reproduced with permission; An extract on p.39 adapted from "Ryanair racism" by Peter Stubley, *The Independent*, 22/1/2018, copyright © The Independent, www.independent.co.uk; A quotation on p.41 by Dr Prun Bijral, **Medical Director of CGL**. Reproduced with kind permission; An extract on p.42 from 'Spice' https://teens.drugabuse.gov/drug-facts/spice, 07/02/2019, National Institute on Drug Abuse; National Institutes of Health; U.S. Department of Health and Human Services; An extract on p.44 adapted from "Ecstasy is getting stronger – and this is what you need to know" by Bobby Palmer, *The Tab*, 2015. Reproduced with permission; An extract on p.51 from 'Diary of a teenage alcoholic' by Nick Webster, *The Mirror*, 20/02/2007, copyright © Mirrorpix, 2007; and an extract on p.61 from https://www.actiononhearingloss.org.uk/, Action on Hearing Loss. Reproduced with permission.

Every effort has been made to trace the copyright holders and obtain permission to reproduce material in this book. Please do get in touch with any enquiries or any information.